GOTTA SING, GOTTA DANCE

BASICS OF CHOREOGRAPHY AND STAGING

By JOHN JACOBSON

Hal Leonard Publishing Corporation

7777 West Bluemound Road P.O. Box 13819 Milwaukee, WI 53213

GETTA SING, GETTA DANCE

INTRODUCTION

It would be impossible to put into a book form accurate and understandable definitions of every dance possibility and staging choice available to a choreographer of song and dance. Fortunately for all of us the possibilities are endless. This book is merely a primer for those individuals who find themselves in the position of wanting to put movements onto their performers. Hopefully, the book can stand on it's own as a catalyst for creativity and the further understanding of an art form that is in a constant state of change and development. Obviously, song and dance is an art of movement that is best demonstrated and understood by a moving educational tool such as a live teacher or at least a video-taped presentation. Therefore, this book will be most effective when used in conjunction with the series of four instructional video tapes also entitled GOTTA SING GOTTA DANCE. The book and the videos are divided into four sections with a different emphasis for each volume. They are:

I. STEP ONE: THE BASICS COME FIRST
II. STEP TWO: PUTTING IT ALL TOGETHER
III. STEP THREE: STAGING THE CONCERT PERFORMANCE
IV. STEP FOUR: MOVEMENT AND STAGING FOR THE YOUNG CHOIR

You will notice that there is a certain amount of review and repetition from one tape to the next because there are many ideas and concepts that are appropriate for more than one of these circumstances. This book is presented to help those that are working on songs and dances to begin to recognize a common language and vocabulary so that we can better communicate our ideas from one to another, to our cast members and ultimately to our audiences. It is in no way the be-all-to-end-all, and does not even presume to be the final authority on the subject. Still, here are some ideas that, with luck, will help make the work of creating songs and dances more manageable and our beautiful art form better equipped to prosper and flourish!

John Jacobson

ABOUT THE AUTHOR

John Jacobson has choreographed, directed and performed in hundreds of staged productions throughout the nation and the world, including Grand Opening Ceremonies for Tokyo Disneyland in Japan, portions of the Macy's Thanksgiving Day Parade, and as choreographer for Ronald Reagan's Inauguration and The Singing Sergeants.

John received his Bachelor's Degree in Choral Music Education from the University of Wisconsin – Madison, where he performed in and eventually directed The Wisconsin Singers. He now holds a Master's Degree in Liberal Arts from Georgetown University. He has served as guest clinician at many national events, including Show Choir Camps of Amercia, the Brightleaf Music Festival, and countless festivals, workshops, music education conferences, and reading sessions throughout the country. The highly successful John Jacobson Workshops are one-day choreography workshops first offered in 1988 under sponsorship of Hal Leonard Publishing Corporation.

John has worked as a consulting writer, choreographer, director and performer for Walt Disney Productions, while conducting seminars for students and music educators on a free-lance basis. He is creator and founder of the non-profit organization AMERICA SINGS! and has authored a video series as well as serving as co-author on a number of published choral revues and musicals, all available through Hal Leonard Publishing Corporation.

THE BASICS COME FIRST

No matter what skill you are trying to learn and perfect, it only makes sense to start from the very beginning with the simplest of concepts. Once mastered, these basic skills become the foundation for growth and even creativity in that field. A basketball player must first learn how to dribble, shoot, pass and pivot before he or she can actually participate in a game. A football player must be able to execute a three point stance, a tackle, a punt-pass-and-kick before he or she can realistically approach the scrimmage line. (In fact, even knowing what the scrimmage line is seems like a bit of basic information.) To work with a computer, a person needs at least fundamental operating skills. To bake a cake, one had best understand the properties of the ingredients to be included. To write in English, one must have a grasp of basic grammatical skills. To design a building, one had better understand the fundamentals of architecture. Likewise, to create, teach and execute dances the creator should begin with a cache of rudimentary skills and a reasonable vocabulary of basic terms from which to proceed. Even a meager amount of experience and familiarity can serve as a catalyst for creativity and more effective teaching of your ideas to others.

AREAS OF THE STAGE

Let's begin with an understanding of the areas of the stage, that is, any stage that you will ever work on. Be it the gym floor of the junior high school, the church basement with a curtain dividing it or the most well-equipped, plush auditorium imaginable, these simple directions are universal.

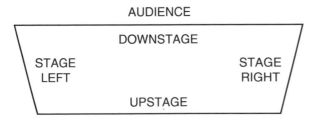

DOWNSTAGE means the area of the stage that is closest to the audience from a proscenium stage. This would usually include anything on that entire half of the stage. However, downstage could also refer to a direction. If you are walking toward the audience you would always be walking "downstage" regardless of whether or not you began your move from a few feet away or from the very back of the stage. Similarly, if a couple of people are facing each other on-stage and the direction is to raise your "downstage" hand, each would raise the hand closest to the audience, precisely one right and the other left.

Downstage hands

UPSTAGE is the opposite of downstage. In other words, this is the area away from the audience in a proscenium arrangement. Likewise, the direction upstage is any movement that is moving away from the audience. The same couple facing each other on stage, with the directive "raise your upstage hand" would raise the hand that is furthest away from the audience.

You may wonder how the terms UPSTAGE and DOWNSTAGE developed. The answer is that stages are sometimes built in what is termed a RAKED formation with the upstage area actually being higher than the downstage area. The entire stage is actually tilting toward the audience. Sometimes this slant is quite steep and at other times hardly noticeable at all. Nevertheless, performers on these stages would actually be walking downhill when moving toward the audience and up hill when moving away from the audience. Subsequently the terms DOWNSTAGE and UPSTAGE are very literal in their meaning. Now, these have become standard terms even on perfectly flat stages.

STAGE LEFT AND STAGE RIGHT — these terms refer to the performer's left and the performer's right as they are facing the audience. This never varies. So you can see that what is the audience's left is still technically STAGE RIGHT and what is the audience's right is technically STAGE LEFT. No matter what direction the performer is actually facing, STAGE LEFT and STAGE RIGHT are the same.

Now you can combine some of these terms to explain more specific areas of the stage. For instance, DOWNSTAGE LEFT would be the quarter of the stage from the audience to mid-stage and from the left edge of the stage to the middle.

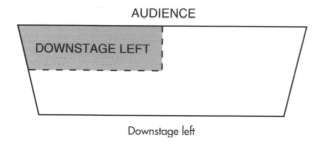

Downstage left

UPSTAGE LEFT would refer to the area from mid stage and back away from the audience and from center stage to the left edge.

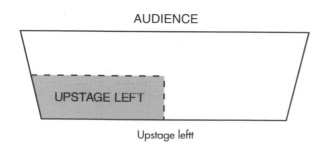

Upstage leftt

Can you find the areas that would be called DOWNSTAGE RIGHT and UPSTAGE RIGHT?

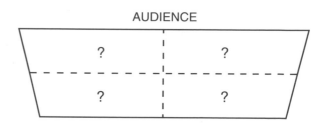

However, since these terms can also refer to a direction as well as an area, a performer far UPSTAGE RIGHT could be said to be moving DOWNSTAGE LEFT even if they are not yet to the quarter of the stage which in area we have deemed DOWNSTAGE LEFT.

Up right to Down left

CENTER STAGE is a line splitting the stage from down to up right through the middle. MID STAGE is a line splitting the stage from left to right through the middle.

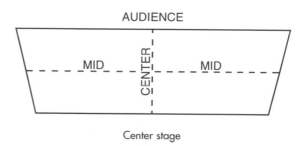

Center stage

BACKSTAGE — This refers to all of the performers' area behind the actual stage itself. This could include dressing rooms, technical areas, etc.

OFFSTAGE — These are the areas of the stage itself which are not visible to the audience.

WINGS — These are side areas of the stage just out of the viewing area of the audience. These are also a part of the OFFSTAGE area.

Just for Practice: Have your performers/students stand in the middle of the stage, even if the stage is simply your class room. Call out directions such as "Point to down stage right" or "Move two steps upstage center." Once your entire cast is comfortable with these basic terms you will greatly reduce the time you usually have to spend explaining simple stage directions. Now, if the entire cast is facing center stage and you tell them to "move their downstage foot" they will automatically know that you mean the left for those on stage left and the right for those on stage right. This can save a lot of time and confusion which often leads to unnecessary frustration.

THE PHENOMENOLOGY OF STAGE AREAS — A final interesting theory about stage areas is the emotional impact certain areas convey to an audience. Through a considerable amount of testing and experimentation some experts have discovered that the strongest area on stage is DOWNSTAGE RIGHT. This is especially true if you are utilizing a soloist in the middle of a larger cast presentation. The theory suggests that a person performing in this area of the stage will portray a sense of strength and confidence to the audience. Perhaps it is because as soon as the audience hears a solo voice they will quickly scan the stage from left to right to find out where that voice is coming from. This is much the same action we would use to read a book. The first place they are going to look is exactly where you have placed your soloist. The second strongest place would be DOWNSTAGE CENTER. According to this theory, where do suppose would be the weakest, or most vulnerable position on-stage? That's right! UPSTAGE LEFT! This is the last place the audiences eyes will come to rest. On occasion you may actually want to have a performer appear to the audience in a weak or vulnerable light. It will be helpful to remember that their position on stage is one important element of establishing this.

Downstage Right

Upstage Left

BODY POSITIONS

Now that we have mastered the "areas of the stage" let's move on to the position of the performer's body upon that stage.

STAGING — refers to positioning performers on the stage and does not necessarily involve any movement once a position has been established. Placing your cast in four rows on choral risers is "Staging." Spreading the cast all over the stage and auditorium, some facing left, right, up, down, is "Staging."

CHOREOGRAPHY — is the art of designing and representing dance. The movement the performers execute individually and as a group is DANCE.

DANCE — is what you do with your body when you move to music.

ZERO POSITION — In order to develop a dance movement we must first establish what is a basic starting posture, or a "Zero position." To do this, stand with your feet comfortably apart, shoulders and arms comfortably down and relaxed. You should display no "attitude," no sense of direction, no musicality.

Now that we have established "Zero" we will discover that every movement or posture other than this is our DANCE.

Zero Position

Pointed Foot

FEET POSITIONS — Let's begin with defining the positions of the dancer's feet.

POINTED — Of course, this means that your toes should be extended as far away from the leg as possible. However, be aware that the instruction "point your toes" is really not the most effective way to create an attractive foot position. The entire foot must be involved. Try turning your heel slightly in as you extend your foot. This will give you an even longer line and a more attractive foot position. Non-trained dancers are most often discovered because of sloppy hand and foot position, so this is an important part of your dance design.

Pointed Foot Turned Out

FLEXED — "Flexed feet" are just the opposite of "pointed feet." A flexed foot includes bringing the toes of the foot as close to the shin as is possible. Again remember that it is the entire foot and not just the toes doing the work. The "flexed" foot is often seen in country western, hillbilly or other character dances.

PARALLEL FEET — This refers to having the heels and toes of one foot exactly the same distance apart and facing in exactly the same way as the other. Very few of us normally stand this perfectly, so that "Parallel feet" may actually be different than the foot position of your "zero" stance and there by constitute a dance choice.

TURNED OUT FEET — Moving from parallel feet, turn your toes out so that they are further apart than your heels.

TURNED IN FEET — Moving from parallel feet, turn your toes in so that they are further apart than your toes. This will give you a "pigeon-toed" look.

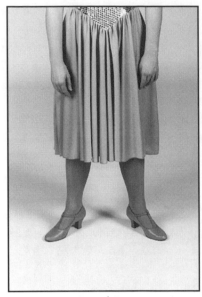

Turned Out

Flexed Foot

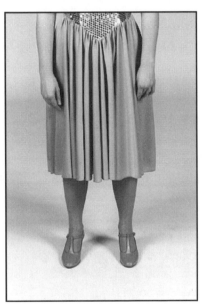

Parallel

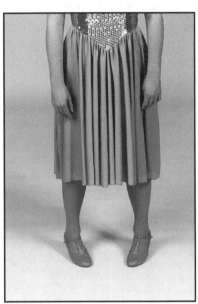

Turned In

In classical ballet and established jazz dance circles, there are a number of clearly defined stances that are universally recognized. Learning this repertoire of terms and the positions they represent can be very useful in song and dance and musical theater venues as well.

FIRST POSITION — Feet together. This can mean that the feet are parallel and together or you can turn the toes out so that just the heels are together. You will want to make sure that your performers know which you have in mind. Usually if the choreographer indicates "first position" they mean that you should stand with your heels together and toes apart. Heels and toes together should include a more specific direction such as "parallel first position," or "first position, heels and toes together."

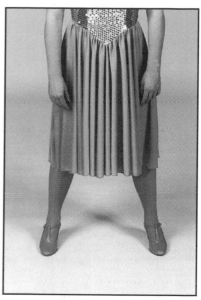
Parallel First Position

Turned Out Second Position – Shoulder Width

SECOND POSITION — Feet apart. Like "first position" there are several variations available for second position. Parallel feet, feet turned in or out are a few of them. There are also various degrees of "feet apart." The choreographer ought to make sure that the dancers are clear as to what is really desired. Specific directions such as "shoulder width," "a comfortable second," or a "wide second" (indicating feet further apart than shoulders) are often included.

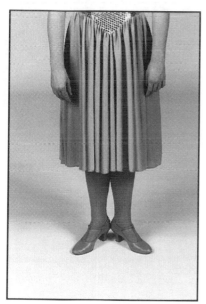
First Position

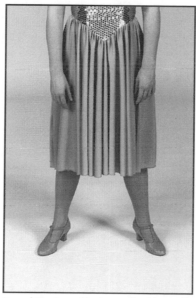
Turned Out Second Position – Shoulder Width

A Comfortable Parallel Second

Wide Second Turned Out

It is generally agreed that a dancer standing in a wide second position is presenting the one of the strongest body language messages possible to the audience. A "narrow" or "casual second" can often send a message that is somewhat weaker, less confident. This is very important to know when analyzing the impact you wish to have on your audience. In many ways, in fact, First Position will send a stronger message than a Narrow Second.

A Strong Second

Weak Second

Fifth Position

Strong First

FIFTH POSITION — Fifth position is mainly used in classical ballet. It involves placing one foot in front of the other with the heel of the front foot between the ball and the big toe of the other foot. The toes of each foot are pointing in opposite directions.

FOURTH POSITION — This is basically the same as fifth position except for the fact that there is some space left between your feet.

Fourth Position

"S" POSE — The "S" POSE is named after the line that can be drawn from shoulder to the floor following the natural contour of the body. One foot is placed in front of the other with the toes of both feet facing the same direction. The dancer's shoulders remain square or parallel to the audience even as the knee of the front foot is facing stage left or right. There are varying degrees of this position with the more extreme looking particularly feminine. This is a pose that is frequently used by models and show girls because it generally is very flattering to the female body. There may be rare occasions that a male dancer would use a version of the "S POSE." You will recognize it as a pose for body builders.

Notice how a less severe "S POSE" can be a very effective way to present a clean line to an entire choir even in a rather traditional choral setting. You will usually be able to tell that if the outside foot of the performers is slightly downstage and closer to center the line of the individual, as well as the entire choir, will be cleaner.

No "S" Pose

"S" Pose

"S" Pose

STAND-BY POSITION — "Stand-by" is a good idea to introduce a degree of discipline and uniformity to your ensemble. It is different from "Zero Position" mainly in that it is an assigned task and thereby a choreographic choice. Your stand-by may be of your own devising. One popular choice, especially with very young performers, is to stand with feet together and hands clasped in the small of your back. The hands should be high enough to leave some space between your ribs and your elbows. This is a very clean and strong position and gets everyone starting in a uniform position. You may want to create your own, unique "stand-by" position. But, here is one choice:

BASIC PARTNERED BALLROOM DANCE POSITION — Of course, there are many ways that two people can stand together: back to back, side to side, front to front, holding hands or not holding hands are just a few. However, a basic ballroom dance position for partners is fairly universal. Facing one another, the gentleman places his right hand on the back waist of his partner and holds her right hand in his left. The woman is holding the gentleman's left hand with her right and has her left hand placed on his back right shoulder. This dance position is like a partnered "stand-by" from which many historical dances begin. Some of these would include the waltz, jitterbug, fox trot, cha cha, lambada and scores of others.

BASIC HAND POSITIONS

One of the most difficult challenges for a choreographer, or a performer for that matter, is what to do with your hands. They are a dead giveaway of nervousness, fatigue or awkwardness. They can be primary indicators of a lack of strength and can be downright distracting when not put under strict control. The best way to overcome these "handy" problems is to give each and every one of them a definite assignment for all periods of performance. This is the job of the choreographer.

"STAND-BY" — The STAND-BY position is one easy choice, in that the hands are behind your back, out of the way of the performer and out of the view of the audience. Your feet ought to be together. Especially with younger performers, try seeing how fast your cast can get into a proper "STAND-BY" position. This can be a lot of fun and a good way to restore order to a chaotic rehearsal or classroom. Have the cast move around and even chatter a little bit and see how fast they can jump into a perfect "Stand-by " position upon your command. STAND-BY is not a great position to stand in for very long, especially if you are trying to maintain a good singing posture. A lot of tension across the chest and rib cage area can occur if your the hands are clasped behind the back for too long. Nevertheless, this can be a good place to begin.

Stand-by Position

Ballroom Dance Position

Other choices for the hands include:

JAZZ HANDS — This hand position, taken from jazz dance really just suggests a wide open hand, fingers spread, palm toward the audience. Try to think of grabbing a huge basketball so that there is a forward curvature to the hand instead of hyper-extending the fingers. This will give your JAZZ HAND a more aggressive look and feel. A REVERSE JAZZ HAND would be essentially the same, except that the palm of the hand would be facing away from the audience.

The JAZZ HAND is used a lot when you want to draw a lot of attention to the hands. They can be very exciting in period music from the '20s to the present. With white or colorful gloves they can be used quite stunningly, almost like a prop. Try them in black light for a novelty effect that is simple yet effective.

Reverse Jazz Hand

BLADES — Blade hands are made with outstretched fingers that are all held tightly together like the "blade" of a knife or sword. It is the kind of hand you might use for a salute, and is very popular with drill teams, because they are easy to make uniform.

FISTS — Fists are tightly closed hands. It is important to realize that fists are traditionally viewed as a gesture and posture of strength. This is a useful tool in dealing with the problem of giving assignments to the hands. If you want your performers to look strong, even when they are just standing still you might try having them all stand with clenched fists. It is difficult to look weak when fists are held in a posture of determination and conviction. Of course, a punched fit into the air is a terrific way to accent a thought. Try using it to accentuate a word like "Rock" (as in "Let's rock!") or words like "Yes!" or even "Hallelujah!" when you want to display a great sense of joy, determination or conviction.

Fists at side

Jazz Hand

Blade Hands

Fist in air

FISTS ON HIPS — Standing with clenched fists on the sides of your hips is usually a very strong posture. It gives a strong message of confidence.

Fists on hips

FISTETTES — FISTETTES, or "Half fists" is just what it says it is. Curl your fingers, but do not clench them all the way into the palm of your hand. It is not as powerful as a full fist but can give a "Funky" feel to a look without being as forceful as a full fist.

JAZZ FISTS ON THE HIP — Standing with jazz hands or clenched fists fastened to the front of your hips can give a strong new line to the dancer's body. This can be used standing still, turning, or moving across the stage. This is generally a good position for singers, as it tends to keep the rip cage high. Again, it is viewed as a position of strength and looks clean on both male and female dancers.

Fistettes

Jazz hands on hips

AT EASE POSITION — This is taken from the military "at ease" command. This is essentially the same as "Stand-by" except that the feet are in a comfortable second position as opposed to being together. Notice what a strong, clean message is being sent by this direct line of the body.

At Ease

RELAXED HANDS AT SIDES WITH SPACE — As simple as it sounds this is not necessarily the easiest of postures to unify and maintain. For even a veteran performer, arms simply dangling at your sides can become uncomfortable and encourages a lot of fidgeting. Still, for a relaxed posture it can appear as the most natural to an audience. Make certain that when you give the direction to stand with your arms at your sides you make it clear that you do not mean arms plastered to your rib cage. There ought to be a natural amount of space between your elbows and your sides to look comfortable and uncor   ' If your young performe.   , a hard time keeping their hands ,o themselves, have them try holding onto the seams of their pants or skirts when their hands are at their sides. Remember, the best way to control the hands is to give them definite assignments.

Hands at sides with space at elbows

Palms up

PALMS UP — What is the message that is being transmitted to your audience when you stand with your palms facing up? It looks as though you are lifting something. It can also suggest words such as "yes," "openness," "generosity," "giving," "happiness," "hope," and many more, usually with a very positive message. It can portray a sense of spirituality, accurately demonstrating a thought such as "Here I am, Lord. I am yours." It says that you are ready to receive something, to catch something, to hold something or to lift something up even if that something is simply an idea or a wish. It is amazing the difference in message a palm up can contribute.

PALMS DOWN — Similarly, PALMS DOWN can give an equally clear message of "no," and "away" and "gone." It can also suggest "Peace," "Tranquillity," "Rest," or "Stop!". When wiping one across the other like a baseball umpire calling a runner "Safe!" PALMS DOWN gives a very strong and clear message of "No!" or "Enough!"

Hands plastered to sides

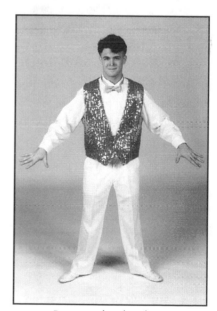
Dancer with palms down

PALMS OUT — This means that the palms of the dancer's hands are facing the audience.

PALMS BACK — This means that the palms of the dancer's hands are facing away from the audience.

When you are trying to make your performers uniform, one of the very first places you should look is at the hands. This is where some of the most obvious discrepancies will be revealed to your audience. Although it is seldom the goal of a creative choreographer to have every performer on stage look exactly alike, since you are dealing with unique human beings with individualities to share, it can often be quite impressive to have a "Rockette-like" degree of precision. The hands are a good place to begin to clean up your act.

If you are wondering why your male dancers don't look as automatically masculine as you would like them to look, examine the assignments that you are giving them for their hands. Probably no single posture is more universally viewed as weak than the "Limp Wrist Syndrome." It is your job as a choreographer to recognize this and fix it. The way to fix it is to give definite assignments to the hands so that it is not left to the dancer's discretion. Tell them to make fists, fistettes, jazz hands, fists to hips or some other specific direction that will help them send the audience the message you have intended through your creation.

BASIC ARM POSITIONS

Now that you've mastered the "art of the hand" let's move on to some basic arm positions that will add to your repertoire of movement.

PRESENT — A "Present" arm is a reference to the move one would make if one were presenting a work of art, a new acquaintance to a gathering or a prize in a game show. The host is said to be "presenting" the person or object that is being introduced. This generally suggests fully outstretched arms with palms up or out. A more specific direction might include the order for Jazz Hands or Blades.

PRESENT LOW — This usually means that the arms are outstretched away from and in front of the body, yet with the hands still below waist level. In most cases the palms would be up with either Jazz or Blade Hands. Further direction might include the degree the arms are lifted in relationship to the body (for instance 90 degrees or 45 degrees).

Present Low arms

PRESENT HIGH — This means that the arms are outstretched up and away from the body above the shoulder level. The hands would usually be blade hands with palms up or Jazz Hands with palms out toward the audience. This is a great pose to end an exciting number or to accent a very important lyric. Again, there can be more specific directions in terms of the degree of height the arms are outstretched.

Present arms — palms up,

Present arms — Jazz hands

18

Present arms — palms down

Fourth Position

JAZZ AND BALLET TRADITIONAL ARM POSITIONS — Classical ballet has given numbers to very specific arm positions that are universally accepted and recognized. In later years, Jazz dance has modified these arm positions. These can be very useful in communicating choices you want your dancers to automatically understand without long verbal explanations or even demonstration.

PRESENT ARMS TO THE AUDIENCE — Try to imagine that the audience is the "prize" that you are presenting. Reach both arms toward them with your palms up. Your hands should be at about chest level, but of course this can vary according to the message you want to send and the audience you want to present.

First Position

Fifth Position

Presenting the audience

Second Position

19

Fifth Position

Notice how the arm positions correspond with the same number positions of the feet.

When combined with other performers, moving or static arm positions can have a predictable effect. There are some moves that have been used so regularly in song and dance that they have developed universally recognized names. One such position is the star burst.

STAR BURST — The STAR BURST consists of a group of dancers all reaching away from the center of their group's body. The dancers in back would reach high. Those on the sides would reach up and/or out. Those in front would reach low and maybe away from the center. It usually works most dramatically if everyone uses strong jazz hands with palms toward the audience, but there are lots of ways to be creative within this basic formation. The STAR BURST is very exciting as a final pose for a song or for a place within the song where a big effect is required. Try making a STAR BURST and then shimmying your hands to make it vibrate. Try growing into the full STAR BURST by keeping your JAZZ HANDS close to your body and slowly moving them to their full extension. This we call an ELASTIC STAR BURST. It can be very effective in demonstrating a crescendo in the music. Experiment with having your STAR BURST expand and retract at varying speeds. Like the opening and closing of a flower it can create a beautiful effect.

SCOOP — An obvious, but useful, direction is the SCOOP. Unlike PRESENTING the scoop is an action more than a position. "SCOOPING your hands from low to high" would indicate a movement from PRESENT LOW to PRESENT HIGH over a period of counts, with palms up as if you were "scooping" up something. Of course, the directions might say SCOOP YOUR LEFT HAND, or SCOOP YOUR RIGHT HAND to indicate independent movement. The directions might even tell you at what level to scoop to or from. For example, "Scoop from low to chest level" would end with a PRESENT AUDIENCE AT CHEST LEVEL.

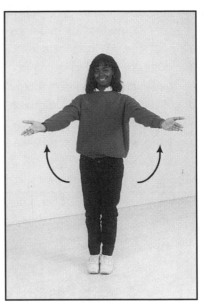

Scoop

Group Starburst

MARCHING ARMS — This would suggest a movement of arms reflective of what you would do if you were marching. It can be performed at varying heights, but most often means elbows bent at 90 degrees and lifted, one at time, to be parallel with the floor at chest level. The arms raise up in opposition to the foot you are marching on. In other words, as you step on your left foot you would raise your right hand and vice versa.

A BUCKET OF WORMS — This is a move that allows the arms to raise up alternately to the left and right, one at a time, always leading with the elbow and allowing the rest of the arm to develop behind it. When a whole group of performers are simultaneously performing this move the result can look like an undulating "BUCKET OF WORMS." Try this move while performing a step-touch. Also try it both standing upright and crouching over so that the arms are actually the highest point of the body at their full extension.

Bucket of worms, standing up

Marching arms

Bucket of worms, bending over

WALKING AND MARCHING

There is a theory that "If you can walk you can dance." The theory goes on to suggest that every single dance step that a choreographer can possibly dream up can, in the end, be broken down into nothing more than creative walking. This actually makes a lot of sense. After all, it is dance "steps" that we are talking about now. Therefore, as we move from building a vocabulary of positions to a creating glossary of moves, the most logical place to start is with the basic human act of "WALKING."

MILITARY MARCH — This is the most standard of march steps. The arms are working in opposition, the left foot is down on the down beat, the arms can be of varying degrees of height from a comfortable walk to 90 degree fists working in strict opposition.

A Military March

HEEL/TOE MARCH — This two-beat march consists of stepping first onto your heel and then continuing onto the rest of the foot. With your feet somewhat turned out this can give a real "Country" look as well as a lively bounce to your walk.

TOE/HEEL MARCH — Another two-beat march that consists of stepping onto the toe first and following with the rest of the foot. This can give a very bouncy and youthful feel, good for popular music as well as funk and swing. Experiment with different arm movements to accompany this march. Try military-style, 90 degree arms as well as elbows tucked into your sides and snapping fingers extended away from the body.

Toe/Heel March

HALF TIME MARCH — Unlike a regular march, the HALF TIME MARCH simply means that you are stepping on beats one and three and skipping two and four. Try this using the 90 degree military march-style arms working in opposition to the foot that you are stepping on. Next, try alternating between a regular speed march and a half time march. The transition between the two is not always as easy as it sounds.

STOP MARCH — This is not to be confused with stopping the march, which basically means to stand still. Instead, a STOP MARCH means to take one marching step only and freeze for anywhere from two to four counts. Both feet are on the floor during this freeze and both hands are down to your sides. In essence, it is a very slow or spread out march with only one step occurring per measure with no movement between the steps. One way to describe it is simply to wind up and stomp one foot every four counts.

SPIRIT OF "76 MARCH — This is a march that is named after the limping steps of a Revolutionary War hero. The march is executed by using the ball of one foot and the flat foot of the other. Now when you march you will get an up-down feel. Try it while pretending to play a fife or flute. Try it while holding a salute. You'll find a lot of use for this on songs like YANKEE DOODLE and WHEN JOHNNY COMES MARCHING HOME.

Spirit of 76 march

COUNTRY WALK/MARCH — To make a regular march look like a country/western dance step, the dancers can turn their knees out as they march like a caricature of an old cowpoke. It adds extra character if you keep your elbows out as well and keep your hands as fists for strength. For variety try slapping your thighs with an open hand on the off beats.

You will find as you progress that much of what makes dance assume the character of a certain era or style is what happens from the waist up. In other words, the dance "steps" themselves become less important than the manner in which they are executed. For instance, a Country Walk is essentially the same as any other marching step except for the fact that you should make a point to turn your knees out, utilize fists and/or slap your thighs on two and four. Of course, there are many other creative ways that you can portray a "country" feel, but this is one that works for sure. What is good to discover is that when you begin to build your vocabulary of dance "steps" to include patterns such as a BOX STEP or a TWO POINT PIVOT you will see that from the waist down many of the characteristic moves are the same. The walking patterns themselves do not make them "Country" or any other style. But, with appropriate upper body modifications those simple routines can translate into any style of music you want them to. Suddenly your vocabulary of moves to draw from will grow very rapidly. You will see this again as we move into period styles like the 1920s, '30s, '50s and '60s, funk, soft shoe, Caribbean and many more!

VAUDEVILLE WALK — Think of the way that a song-and-dance man like Danny Kay, Dick Van Dyke, or for that manner Jimmy Durante and Bugs Bunny enter the stage with a hat in one hand and a cane under the opposite arm. The walk is very stiff and straight legged. If there are no props the arms, too, are as straight as possible swinging in opposition to the leg that you are stepping onto. This step is very effective for an individual or for an entire line of dancers to make their way on or off the stage.

The Vaudeville Walk

CHARLIE CHAPLIN WALK — There are many dance steps that were made famous, or perhaps invented, by the personalities that used them in their acts. Consider "THE CURLY SHUFFLE" or "THE SOUPY SHUFFLE," one made famous by Curly, of The Three Stooges, the next by the famous actor/comedian Soupy Sales. The CHARLIE CHAPLIN WALK is one such universally-recognized step. You can just see that legendary actor with his heels together and toes apart walking along like a penguin, swinging a watch chain or an umbrella in one hand, the other at his side or grasping the lapel of his tailed coat.

The Charlie Chaplin Walk

DANCE STEPS

Now that you have mastered the art of walking, and perhaps walking in unison with the rest of the cast, you will be able to modify that walking into different patterns on the floor and create more sophisticated dance routines. You will soon discover that most dance routines are nothing more complicated than walking in different patterns, with the character and variety developing from the rest of the body. Here are some basic dance steps whose names are recognized by dancers and choreographers of all degrees of experience and from most genres of the medium.

BALL CHANGE — This means changing the weight from the ball of one foot onto the other foot. You will very often see the direction "Step, Ball Change." This simply directs you to step fully onto one foot then step onto the ball of the other foot and quickly back to the original. The rhythmic pattern is a dotted eighth note followed by a sixteenth and a quarter note.

♫ ♩

1 & 2

KICK, BALL CHANGE — Another familiar pattern is "Kick, ball change." This involves kicking one foot on beat one followed by stepping onto the ball of the other foot and immediately returning the weight to the original foot. As an exercise try doing several "step, ball changes" then "kick, ball changes" in succession. One of the very important things to remember is that there are no touches in this pattern. Instead, there are complete weight changes with every move. You will often see beginner dancers not transferring their entire weight onto the ball of the second foot for the "ball" part of the "ball change." Essentially, the move is walking in a different rhythmic pattern. Normally we do not interrupt our walking with intermittent touches but complete weight changes.

JAZZ SQUARE/BOX STEP — These are two names for the same step, absolutely interchangeable. The JAZZ SQUARE or BOX STEP is nothing more than four marching or walking steps in a new pattern on the floor. However it can be executed in a variety of ways to adapt to many styles of music. One of the reasons it is so popular is that it can look quite sophisticated even though it is easy to accomplish. Also, it is a dance step that manages to keep the performer always facing the audience and thus, is very conducive to song and dance where it is very important to keep the singer's voice consistently toward the audience. A basic JAZZ SQUARE or BOX STEP is executed by stepping straight ahead with one foot (let's say the left). Follow this with the right foot stepping across and in front of that left. Thirdly, you step again onto your left foot, back and then again onto your right foot exactly where you begin. So, you see that after four complete steps you have not moved from where you began.

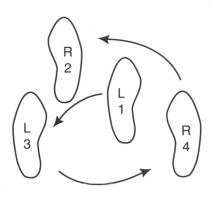

The box step

Try practicing several of these in a row. What modifications can you make to your upper body to make your BOX STEP look more "Country?," "Funky?," "Military?"

Another way to give this step a different look and feel is to begin it with the cross over step on one. Then, step two is the left foot stepping back. Three is the right foot again back to where it started and four is the left foot stepping forward. Try each of these versions several times. Do you see how you could add even more variety by beginning with the third step on one? or even the fourth?

Try the BOX STEP again. This time as you cross the right foot over bend your knees so that your entire body dips down on two. Try several of these in a row, always adding the dip on step two and straightening up on three, four and one.

Now that you have mastered the box step beginning on the left foot, try it on the opposite side. This is simply beginning the pattern with the right foot on one. Step straight ahead, cross the left foot over, step back on the right for count three and back to your beginning position by stepping onto the left foot on four.

Can you make your JAZZ SQUARES look more "Jazzy" by snapping your fingers on the offbeat? How about spreading your fingers in wide jazz hands and making your SQUARES resemble a dance of the 1920s?

Box Step – 3

The Box Step – 1

Box Step – 4

Box Step – 2

DOUBLE JAZZ SQUARE OR BOX STEP — Now that you have mastered a BOX STEP to both the left and the right, let's try to put the two of them in succession. A DOUBLE BOX STEP is simply one BOX STEP to the left followed immediately by a BOX STEP to the right with a quick BALL CHANGE in between. The counts would be:

1	(L)
2	(R)
3	(L)
4&	(RL)
1	(R)
2	(L)
3	(R)
4	(L)

Do several DOUBLE BOX STEPS in a row. Now make your DOUBLE BOX STEPS "Country," "1920s," "Swing," "Military," etc.

PLIÉ — This is a French term that means "bend your knees." DEMI-PLIÉ means "half plié" and means to bend your knees or squat about halfway to the floor. GRAND PLIÉ means to bend your knees to their full extent, lowering yourself almost to the floor.

Demi Plié

Grand Plié

RELÉVE — is generally considered to be the opposite of plié, and means that you are standing with your heels off the floor onto your toes or the balls of your feet.

Plié and Reléve are both a position and an action. "Standing in plié" means that you are standing with your knees bent, or you may be told to "plié" which would means to bend your knees. Likewise, a person could be "standing in reléve" which is a position, or they could be told to "reléve" which would be the action of rising up from the heels.

The feet are the first of what some people would call our human "elevators." These allow us to create new pictures with added height. The knees are the second of those "elevators" which give us degrees of depth in our movements and our stage pictures.

PIVOTS — another stepping pattern on the floor gives us the TWO and FOUR POINT PIVOTS.

The TWO POINT PIVOT is a 4-count step that amounts to stepping forward on one foot (let's say left) on beat 1. On 2, the dancer steps with their right foot toward the back of the stage facing in that direction. In other words, you have now turned 180 degrees to your right and are facing upstage. The third step is again the left and goes straight upstage. The fourth continues you around to the right so that you are again facing the front. Remember that each count is a step. There are no touches or half pirouettes. Also, once you begin turning in one direction there is no reversing the action. The entire two point pivot is executed turning either to the left or the right, not half and half. The term TWO POINT comes from the two pivot points with the four steps, one to the front and one to the back.

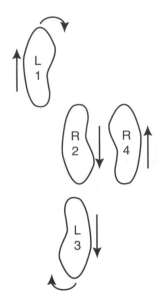

Two point pivot

Try doing several TWO POINT PIVOTS in a row. You may want to put four to twelve marching steps in between each pivot as you rehearse. Try some two point pivots beginning with the right foot and turning to your left.

Two point pivots are a great way to change character within a song or medley. As you briefly turn your back on the audience you can become a new character or change the mood of the song you are performing. The ends of phrases that end with either a whole note or a quarter and three counts of rest are good places to try out a precise TWO POINT PIVOT.

FOUR POINT PIVOT — This pattern on the floor takes eight steps as opposed to the four of the previous pattern. It contains four pivot points, each of the four walls of the stage, as opposed to two. Step forward with your left foot and pivot to face the right while stepping onto your right. Step toward the stage right wall with your left foot on three and pivot to face upstage while stepping onto your right foot on four. On five, step upstage with your left foot and pivot to face stage left while stepping onto your right foot. Step toward stage right on your left foot for the count of seven, pivoting back to the front and stepping onto your right foot for the eighth and final count.

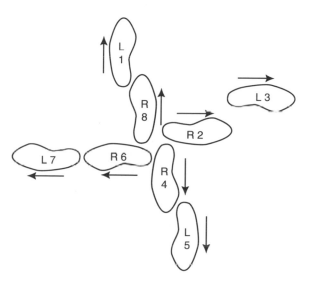

Four point pivot

Try several four point pivots in a row. You may want to put eight counts of marching in between each one to re-orient yourself. Try not to look at the floor as your execute the steps. Trust that, as usual, it is there.

Try a pattern of marching that is interspersed with TWO and FOUR POINT PIVOTS. One pattern might be:

12 marches - 1 two point turn - 8 marches - 1 four point pivot - 12 marches - 1 two point pivot - 8 marches - 1 four point pivot

Can you think of a song that would work with this marching pattern? Try "I'M A YANKEE DOODLE DANDY." How about "OH WHEN THE SAINTS GO MARCHING IN?"

As before, think of upper body modifications which would make this pattern look country, military, swing, 1920s, etc.

LUNGE PIVOT — A LUNGE PIVOT is exactly the same as a two point pivot except that you make more of a production out of the first step than you do out of steps two, three and four. On one, step forward with your left foot just as you did in the TWO POINT PIVOT. At the same time burst your jazz hands from high to low in one count. Leave them at your sides for the next three counts. This can be a very explosive move and very exciting to watch. Try it with lunges both on steps one and three, with the arm bursts happening first down stage and then up.

Have several lines of dancers do PIVOT BURSTS beginning two counts apart for an exciting sequential effect. Try some PIVOT BURSTS beginning with the right foot and turning to your left.

Pivot burst 1

Pivot burst 2

Pivot burst 3

Pivot burst 4

Try some other variations of the LUNGE portion of a LUNGE PIVOT. For instance, try pointing your left hand at the audience as you step forward for count one of your pivot. How about punching your right fist up in the air at an angle over the audiences head on the lunge. The hands can still return to your sides for counts two through four, or you can think of another creative way to add them to the routine.

TURNS — Simple turns in a dance routine need not be difficult or intimidating to be effective audience pleasers.

PIROUETTES — These are spins or twirls usually on one foot or the other, and generally in one place. Of course you can make a single, double, triple or more out the turn but the definition is the same. To be a bit more descriptive, a PIROUETTE will sometimes be more specifically described as INSIDE or OUTSIDE.

An example of an INSIDE PIROUETTE would be to spin to your right on your left foot, or to spin to your left on your right foot.

Inside Pirouette

An example of an OUTSIDE PIROUETTE would be a turn to your right on your right foot or a spin to your left on your left foot.

Outside Pirouette

A TWO-FOOTED PIROUETTE would describe a turn in either direction with both feet keeping constant contact with the floor. A more specific direction might include A TWO-FOOTED PIROUETTE in PLIÉ or RELÉVE indicating with "bent knees" or "on your toes."

THREE POINT TURNS — This describes a turn that uses four counts and three turning points to complete. It also suggests that the dancer is moving in the direction that the turn is going. A "three point turn to the left" would have the dancer traveling at least some distance to the left. A "three point turn to the right" would take them further stage right as long as they began the move facing the audience. One could actually do a "three point turn to the left" that took you closer to the audience as long as the step was instigated by a dancer facing stage right at the onset.

To practice a THREE POINT TURN simply face front with the weight on your right foot. Now step to the left on "one." By count two you will have made a half turn to your left and will be facing upstage. Step three is completed by stepping onto your left foot again having completed the turn so that you are again facing front, however somewhat more to stage left than where you began. Count four can either be a touch of the right foot or a pause.

Try a THREE POINT TURN to the left followed immediately by another to the right so that you are back to where you started. Try several in PLIÉ and several in RELÉVE. Experiment with creative ways to fill up count four. Clap, snap, jump, slide. What else?

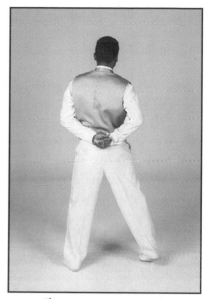

Three point pivot — step 2

Three point pivot — step 1

Three point pivot — step 3

CIRCLE AROUND YOURSELF — Like most dance steps that have names this one is exactly what it says it is. In any number of counts, the dancer takes a little stroll in a circle around nothing but him or herself. Like a TWO POINT PIVOT this can be a great opportunity to change character within a song or medley. Notice the flowing motion that happens on the stage when an entire cast walks around themselves all at the same tempo and the same direction. Try a CIRCLE AROUND YOURSELF in four counts, eight counts, twelve counts. Try a small, tight circle. Try a circle that covers a bigger portion of the stage. Try walking in a CIRCLE AROUND YOURSELF and at the same time keep your face toward the audience for as long as possible and then quickly snap it around to the other side as you almost have completed the circle. This is called "spotting." Try skipping in a CIRCLE AROUND YOURSELF. Try jogging, tip-toeing, skating or other interesting ways of making this into a real dance step.

CIRCLE AROUND YOUR PARTNER — When accomplished with both of the participants facing the audience for the entire revolution this is called a DO SI DO. Taken from square dancing, it can none-the-less be used in a variety of other settings as well. Again, try skipping a DO SI DO, then running, then skating. Try a pattern where you do not have to keep facing the audience for the entire pattern. Add a third person to your couple and try to extend your CIRCLE AROUND YOUR PARTNER to a FIGURE EIGHT PATTERN.

STEP HOP — So far, all of the steps that we have discussed have been nothing more than glorified walking. This is definitely true of the BOX STEP, the TWO POINT PIVOT, THE FOUR POINT

PIVOT and THE CIRCLE AROUND YOURSELF and CIRCLE AROUND YOUR PARTNER. You will discover as we go along that there are a lot more ways of walking than the one we all take for granted. It makes doing choreography a lot more interesting and dancing a lot more comprehensible.

If you were to simply add a "hop" in between each "step" you would have a whole new array of dances to draw from. A STEP HOP means to step fully onto one foot and then hop on that same foot. Follow it with the same routine to the other side and using the other foot. As before the versatility of a STEP HOP will become evident when you begin to add the upper body postures and gestures that reflect a period, style or lyric.

One finger in the air, the other hand on the hip added to a STEP HOP becomes a Truckin' Step reminiscent of the 1940s and '50s. Stiffed-legged STEP HOPS, swinging from one foot to the other and clapping on two and four can be an enthusiastic audience getter for songs like PREPARE YE THE WAY OF THE LORD from GODSPELL or AMEN from LILIES OF THE FIELD. Try the same stiffed-legged STEP HOP with a partner in traditional ballroom dance position and you have a great CHARLESTON or RAGTIME dance!

Truckin' Step-hop

Hop clap

Partner step hop

STEP TOUCH — A Step Touch is nothing more than a "half-time" march with a "touch" on the two and four beats of the measure. It is the first step that we are learning that does not involve a weight change, but instead keeps the weight on the foot that you have stepped onto until after the touch is completed. To teach STEP TOUCHES, have the cast march in unison and in place. Then change from a regular march to a half-time march. Third, add the touches on two and four so that the dancers are moving back and forth as opposed to the up and down motion of a regular march.

Now you will be ready to make the modifications to this very basic move that will give it the character of a variety of dances.

SWAY SNAPS — The easiest dance step of all is probably the SWAY SNAP. It is easy because every thing is going in the same direction. Teach it by having the cast members stand on their right foot with both hands off to the right with slightly bent elbows. As you step to the left let your hands

swing in a "U" pattern to the left side. Snap your fingers as you touch the floor with your right foot on "two." Repeat this same pattern to the right stepping on three, touching left and snapping on "four."

Sway snap 1

Sway snap 2

FUNKY STEP TOUCH BEHIND — This can be achieved by stepping well out to the side on "one" and touching with the right foot behind and to the left of the left foot on "two" all the time keeping your shoulders square to the audience. Notice how the elbows and "Fistettes" give an added dimension and funky attitude to this STEP TOUCH.

Funky step touch behind - step 1

Funky step touch behind - step 2

FUNKY STEP TOUCH IN FRONT — Again step out to the left on "one" and then touch or dig the heel of your right foot into the ground in front of your left foot on "two." The elbows and fistettes can lift up on "one" and push down in opposition to the "digging" foot on two for a very strong and funky feel.

COUNTRY STEP TOUCHES — What are the characteristic elements that you will want to add to a step touch to make it look particularly COUNTRY in nature? If you said "elbows out," "flexed feet," "fists or slapping open hands on your thighs on the off beats," you were absolutely right!

U-STEP — A "U-step" is a step touch in which you keep your shoulders square to the audience and make a dipping motion as you step touch. The pattern has a down-up pattern like that of the letter "U." This step works well with music that is in "three" or in a feeling of "one" like a minuet or a hesitation waltz. Begin by stepping to the left on the left foot from plié to reléve as the right foot comes along to touch by count "two." The third beat of the three count pattern can actually be a "hold" or "freeze" with feet together in reléve.

Try some "U-STEPS" to a song like CHIM CHIM CHEREE, LET'S GO FLY A KITE or any waltz that suits your fancy. Try some "U-STEPS" lightly with bounce on top of the floor for a happy song like ZIP-A-DEE-DOO-DAH, or into the floor hardly coming out of your plié at all for songs like HE'S A TRAMP or BASIN STREET BLUES.

Funky step touch in front - step 1

Country step touch 1

Funky step touch in front - step 2

Country step touch 2

U-Step 1

Cakewalk — Individual

U-Step 2

Cakewalk — Partners

touches will go directly back from the dancer's main frame. Try four to the front followed immediately by four to the back. Cut it down now so that there are only two step touches to the front and two to the back. Eventually, make the change so that you are only doing one step touch to the front followed by one to the back. Keep this pattern going and you will find yourself doing the famous CHARLESTON, which by now you understand is nothing more than step touching in different patterns on the floor, which by now you realize is nothing more than half time walking!

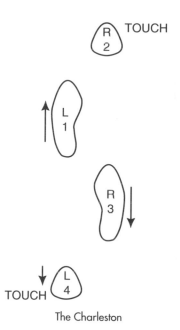

The Charleston

CAKEWALK STEP TOUCH — Hop onto your left foot from your right on "one" and then lightly touch your pointed right foot out to the right side on "two." Repeat to the other side for an elegant CAKEWALK step touch. This can be accomplished as an individual or as partners, with the gentleman standing behind the woman and holding both her hands or one hand and her waist. The same foot would be stepped on and the same one touched in this simultaneous partnered CAKEWALK STEP TOUCH.

CHARLESTON — One of the most fun dances that ever came out of the 1920s, in fact the dance that we most regularly associate as dance of that era, is the CHARLESTON. This high energy dance has countless variations but is essentially nothing more than a series of "step touches." The step touches are executed first to the front and then to the back. To teach the step to beginner dancers have them start by repeating a number of step touches in place with each of the touches being placed directly in front of you. Then practice a series of the same except that the

Now you are ready to add the upper body movements and hand gestures that will give your basic CHARLESTON step real character.

As simplistic as some of this may sound it is crucial that we teach these basic dance steps with a square one approach to the fundamentals. How easy it will seem to your beginner cast members to perform a Charleston once they get the connection between it and a move they can all do without thinking, namely "walking."

33

GRAPEVINES — Grapevines are another variety of dance steps that look difficult but are actually as easy as putting one foot in front of the other. They can be of any length, speed or rhythm that the choreographer desires and that the dancers can execute. On all of them the shoulders are kept square to the audience. The hands and arms can be adjusted to suit any style of music you can imagine, fists and elbows for country/western, conga arms for music of the Caribbean, palms down as if they were resting on a table for a soft-shoe, jazz hands up and facing the audience for a wild Charleston, and low snaps for swing or jazz are just a few of the possibilities. What you do with your feet is essentially the same for all of these grapevines.

FOUR COUNT GRAPEVINE — Begin by understanding that a FOUR COUNT GRAPEVINE is four marching steps in a new pattern on the floor. So, practice those four steps in place (left, right, left, right). Now, take the first left and step out to the left side on "one." Step "two" involves stepping on the right foot in front of the left continuing the movement left. Count "three" is the left foot again stepping out to the left side and step "four" is bringing the right foot together with the left, or touching its heel out to the right side. Reverse the FOUR COUNT GRAPEVINE by stepping to the right beginning on the right foot and following with the left in front then right behind and left together. Practice this routine several times with each step getting the same time value, quarter notes, for instance. Once the step is mastered, experiment with giving the four counts a dotted rhythmic pattern.

♪   ♩.   ♪   ♩.
L   R   L   R (heel)

MOVING LEFT
←

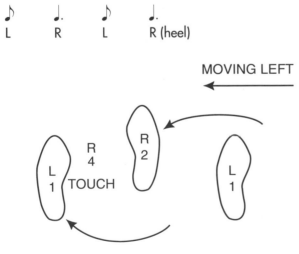

Four count grapevine

Now you are ready to experiment with what to do with your hands during a FOUR COUNT (SHORT) GRAPEVINE.

1. Make JAZZ HANDS with your palms out to the audience. Cross your hands when your feet cross and keep them open when your feet are not crossed. In other words, your hands will be crossed on beat two. This will give you a good Charleston or Vaudeville look.

2. Try the same crossing motion but with your palms down as if they were resting on a desk or table. This will give the look of a soft shoe.

3. Fists in this same pattern will make your FOUR COUNT GRAPEVINES look tough and Country.

4. "Traveling Arms" (like the signal a referee uses to call "traveling!" in a basketball game) will give it a Conga look.

5. Put your hands in your front or back pockets for a relaxed and uncluttered look.

Four count grapevine — beat 2

Four count grapevine — beat 4

You can certainly see that there will be a lot of use for a FOUR COUNT GRAPEVINE in any style of song and dance!

EIGHT COUNT (LONG) GRAPEVINE — Essentially the same as a four count grapevine, the EIGHT just takes it a little further. At the risk of over stating this technique, be reminded again that, like the FOUR, even an EIGHT COUNT GRAPEVINE is simply walking or marching in a different pattern on the floor. Practice eight steps in place. Now, moving continually to the left, the eight steps go in a pattern that is:

1 Left - step out and to the side
2 right - step in front of the left foot
3 left - step out again to the left
4 right - step behind the left foot
5 left - step out and to the left
6 right - step again in front of the left
7 left - step out again to the left
8 right - bring the feet together, or touch the right heel out to the right.

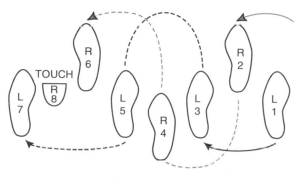
Eight count grapevine

Reverse the entire eight counts starting with your right foot and moving continuously to the right. Practice it until it is comfortable in an even eight pattern and then try it with dotted rhythms like this:

♪ ♩. ♪ ♩. ♪ ♩. ♪ ♩.
L R L R L R L R (heel)

Then, reverse that pattern beginning with your right foot and moving continuously to the right.

Now, experiment with the same variety of arm and hand movements that you used for the FOUR COUNT GRAPEVINE to create a variety of looks and styles using only this one eight count routine.

CHUGS — These are dance moves that are used a lot in the Charleston and could be put to some use in popular and even country/western dance. A CHUG is simply jumping with both feet into the floor at the same time in one direction. Bend your knees as you do so, so that the move is almost like skidding to a halt. Try using JAZZ hands at shoulder level as you jump to accent the move.

Chug

BACKSTEP — A BACKSTEP consists of two walking steps, one behind the other. The action is a rocking motion that is usually a preparation for another dance pattern.

As an exercise try combining a few of the walking patterns that you have learned so far to get the feeling of the weight change of a BACKSTEP. For instance, kick your left foot straight out in front and then step back on it and forward on the right. Try this several times in succession:

1-2	Kick (L)
3-4	Backstep (LR)
1-2	Kick (L)
3-4	Backstep (LR)
1-2	Kick (L)
3-4	Backstep (LR)

After you have mastered this side try it to the other side, kicking the right foot and BACKSTEPPING on the right/left. Notice how there can be two counts for the kick and one for each step so that you fill up a four count measure. If you gave the kick and each step only one count you would have a kick, backstep that would fill a three count measure giving you a new step to use in a 3/4 dance such as the WALTZ.

There is very little difference between a BACKSTEP and a BALL CHANGE except that a BALL CHANGE is usually a dotted rhythm giving the "ball" of the step less time value than the step.

Another exercise to practice your BACKSTEPS is simply to march in place for six even steps and then make counts seven and eight a BACKSTEP. Repeat that pattern several times to get the feeling of the difference in weight change between marching and backstepping.

STEP KICK — Step on one foot and follow it with a kick of the other. Like most well named dance steps this one is exactly what it's name suggests.

Moving from the world of "STEP TOUCH" into the world of the "STEP KICK" may seem like not such a big deal. After all, by now you are realizing that even a STEP KICK must be nothing more than STEP TOUCHES with the touch being in the air. And we all know that step touches are nothing more than half time WALKING.

However, the huge new array of dance moves that are available to you once you have mastered the STEP KICK make this transition very exciting and makes your "bag of tricks" grow profoundly!

How many ways can you imagine to modify a basic STEP KICK to give it new and varied character? Can you make it fit a Country Dance? A Cakewalk? A Jitterbug? Here are just a few of the options easily accessible to you.

STEP KICK ALA KICKLINE — Notice that the instruction given to you in the very name of the step tells you to step first and then kick. This will always make the accenting "kick" hit on beats two and four for a rousing routine. Notice how different the dance would look and feel it you kicked first and then stepped. This is another option now available to you. Try your STEP KICKS at varying heights and speeds. Try them as an individual and in a line up like the famous RADIO CITY ROCKETTES who have made STEP KICKING their trademark.

Step Kick

Try the STEP KICK without fully extending your kicking foot, rather just lifting your knee in a high stepping "HINGE."

Step Hinge

The ROCKETTES famous "Eye-High" kicks are usually performed straight at the audience. Since most of us are neither shaped like nor can kick as high as the ROCKETTES, try having your STEPKICKS go from side to side. Try some at knee level. How about waist level? O. K., go ahead and kick as high as your eye and then go soak your hamstrings! Make sure to point your foot as this will make your leg look longer and straighter.

Try having all of your STEP KICKS go toward downstage left even though your shoulders are square to the audience.

Now try them all to stage right, even as you are alternating feet with each kick.

Try doing three STEP KICKS down stage left followed by three STEP KICKS down stage right with a BACKSTEP in between. Repeat this "eight count" pattern several times for an interesting twist to your KICKLINE.

FOUR COUNT STEP KICKS WITH THE DEVELOPING KNEE
1 - Step Left.
2 - Lift your bent right knee almost to waist level toward downstage left.
3 - Straighten your right knee toward down stage right.
4 - Bend again that right knee

Repeat to the other side using the left leg for the kicking.

4-Count Step kick - step 1

4-Count Step kick - step 3

4-Count Step kick - step 2

4-Count Step kick - step 4

CHARLESTON STEP KICK — This high kick is almost like what a punter does in a football game.
1 - Step with one foot (L).
2 - Follow with a high kick as you arms swing way above your head (R).
3 - Step back with your kicking foot (R).
4 - Touch your original stepping foot (L) back as far as it can go as the opposite hand (R) touches the floor.

Charleston step kick - step 3

Charleston step kick - step 1

Charleston step kick - step 4

Try this same step beginning with the opposite foot.

Charleston step kick - step 2

HOP KICK — This is almost the same as a STEP KICK, except that the dancer is jumping onto the "stepping" foot instead of "stepping." This is going to give the dance a much more energetic look and a totally different feel than the STEP KICK.

Try some HOP KICKS low and across the front for a move that will feel appropriate for "swing" or faster for "Charleston" or "Ragtime" music.

Hop kick

Try to hop a number of times on one foot and kick the opposite foot low and across the front on each of the off beats. For example try this pattern four times kicking the right foot, then four times kicking the left foot. Follow this with two of each, and finally with one of each four times. In other words: 4R-4L-2R-2L-1L-1R-1R-1L. This will be a fun pattern to incorporate in a variety of energetic dance routines.

COUNTRY HOP KICKS (A)

1 - Hop onto your left foot while at the same time bringing your right foot behind your knee.

2 - On beat two, kick that right leg out to your right.

3 - Step on that right leg for beat three with the left leg coming behind.

4 - On four, kick your left leg out to the left side.

Don't forget to flex your feet and use your fists to make this step look very COUNTRY.

Country hop kick - 1

Country hop kick - 2

COUNTRY KICK (B) — Another Country-looking HOP KICK would be to hop onto the left foot and simultaneously kick the right flexed foot out to the right side. Then on beat two, jump onto the right foot and simultaneously kick the left foot out to the left. It is really nothing more than running in place except that you are really kicking up your heels as you do so. In this dance step, the hop and the kick happen at the same time. Try about eight of these in a row for an easy and yet impressive Country/Western dance that is, at the same time, masculine and fun.

Country Kick

FALL KICKS

1 - Fall onto your left foot as though you were going to run toward stage left.

2 - Twist your right leg at the knee and kick that right foot out to the right side.

3 - Fall onto the right foot as if you were going to run to stage right.

4 - Twist your left leg and kick it out to the left side as you had done with the right on beat 2.

Try several of these in a row for a cute character dance.

Fall kick - 1

Fall kick - 2

BELL KICKS — This is another name for jumping up in the air, both legs off to one side and clicking your heels together. The name "Bell Kick" comes from the shape of your bowed legs off to the side as the heels kick together and the swinging motion from side to side as you perform several of these kicks in a row. BELL KICKS look very difficult and impressive to an audience but are, in truth, not hard at all. The way to learn them is to practice step kicking alternately to each side. The "step" should first come across the front on beat "one" (use your left foot to practice. On "two" lift or kick your right foot out to the side with a flexed foot. On "three" step across again this time with your right foot in front of the left. On "four" lift or kick the left foot out to the left with a flexed foot. Try these four counts several times in a row to get the rhythm of the BELL KICK.

Practice Bell kick - 2

Now, practice (perhaps using a friend or a wall for support) doing the first two counts and freezing with your right leg suspended in the air. Leave that foot there and try bringing the left heel up to meet it for a click in the air. MOST DANCERS MAKE THE MISTAKE OF TRYING TO BRING THE RIGHT LEG DOWN TO MEET THE LEFT. THIS DOES NOT WORK. The left leg, or the bottom leg in either case, is the leg that is really doing most of the work.

Now you are ready to try a full BELL KICK, which you realize are nothing more than step touches with the touch happening in mid air!

Bell kick

Practice Bell kick - 1

Assisted Bell kick

40

CUTAWAYS — These are another version of a step kick with very exciting results -

1 - Jump onto your left foot while at the same time bringing your right foot behind the left knee.

2 - On "two" kick that right foot out to the right.

3 - On "Three" jump onto the right foot while bringing the left foot behind the right knee.

4 - On "four" kick that left foot out to the left side.

Cross your arms when your legs are crossed, in other words on "one" and "three," and "Present" them low when you are doing the kick out to the side (on "two" and "four").

Cutaway - step 1

Cutaway - step 2

STEP KICK AS A SLOW LEG LIFT — Try alternating leg kicks that are less an actual "kick" than they are a simple lifting of the leg to one side or the other across the front. Think of this step in a count of three. (1) On one step left. (2-3) For beats two and three simply lift your straight right leg across the front. Then step right and lift the left leg for two counts across the front of the right. This can be quite a beautiful step kick in a waltz pattern.

CHASSÉ — A Chassé is really just a slide to one side or the other involving three steps in a dotted rhythm. Practice sliding left.

♩.   ♪   ♩
L   R   L

Practice to the right.

♩.   ♪   ♩
R   L   R

Now try combining a CHASSÉ and the STEP KICK that is really a lift of the leg. Chassé left followed by a lift of the right leg across the front. Chassé right followed by a step lift of the left leg across the front of the right leg.

Chassé

Lift right leg

The next two steps are basic tap dance terms every dancer needs to know.

FLAP — To "flap" your foot brush it forward, scuffing the ball and toes of the foot on the ground as you go and then immediately put weight on that foot to stop the move. It should even make a sound like FL...AAAP! Keep the weight off from your heels at all times on this step.

SHUFFLE — A shuffle begins the same way as a FLAP, in that you brush the foot forward. However in this case you also brush the foot back so that their are still two sounds but no change of weight. Like the FL...AAAP the SHUFFLE sounds like its name. The two sounds should be as even and clear as the word SHUF....FLE.

Practice these two steps over and over and over. That is the only way to make them become second nature to you and your feet!

RECOGNIZABLE STEPS THAT ACTUALLY HAVE NAMES!
To end this first lesson here are a few steps or moves that you have probably seen dancers perform at one time or another and wondered "how did they do that ?" "What is that move called?" or "I wonder how I could use that in my show?" And even if you didn't here they are...

KNEE POPS FROM SECOND POSITION — Standing with your feet in a "wide second position" quickly bend your knees forward by raising up onto your toes. Do this without letting the level of your head go either up or down. Heels back down as the legs straighten out on beat "two." This can be a fun move, especially for the men in your cast. Try it on every other beat for a couple of lines of songs like "HELLO MY BABY," a sea chantey or western song.

Knee pop

SUGAR FOOT — No this is not a sweet monster that haunts the heights of the Himalayas. Instead it is a nifty walking dance step of the '30s through '50s. Begin by walking in place while at the same time twisting on the balls of your feet in the same direction. Both feet point left then both point right. It should be as if you are squishing something with your feet.

1. Try the SUGARFOOT moving forward.
2. Try it moving in a circle around yourself.
3. Try it holding onto the right hand of a partner with your right hand and staying in one place.
4. Now try to turn in a circle with your partner as you do the SUGARFOOT.

Sugarfoot

SHIM SHAM or FLIM FLAM — These are two names for the same step taken from the 1930s and 1940s.

Begin with your feet together and keep them flat to the floor, when you step the entire foot steps at once.
(A) Step with the left foot out and drag it back to where it started. (1-2)
(B) Do the same with the right foot. (3-4)
(C) Repeat with the left foot. (5-6)
(D) Beat "and 7" is a BALL CHANGE (R L) and repeat the step with the left.
(E) Drag back of the left foot. (8)

Repeat the entire eight count pattern beginning with the right foot.

THE LINDY — The Lindy is a very popular dance step from the '30s through the '50s and still performed in a lot of clubs and dance halls all over the world. Learn the basic four count dance pattern as an individual first and then put it together with a dance partner for a very lively, smooth and versatile dance step.

THE LINDY involves five walking steps with a unique pattern on the floor. The first three are really a CHASSÉ in one direction (say left). That is, L-R-L in a dotted rhythm moving to the left with the shoulders square to the audience. This is followed by a back step (R L). Then slide to the right with the same CHASSÉ (R L R) pattern followed by a backstep (L R). You have just completed two full LINDY steps. Try several of these in a row to music like IN THE MOOD or TUXEDO JUNCTION.

Eventually, you will see how the LINDY step can be used with turns and spins, passes and lifts to make a very sophisticated and spirited routine!

The Lindy

JITTERBUG — The Lindy's close first cousin is the traditional JITTERBUG dance step. The JITTERBUG is usually a six count pattern that will mercifully bring you back to square one after 24 counts of dancing. The pattern is:

Toe heel L (1-2)
Toe heel R (3-4)
Back step L R (5-6)

In a ballroom dance position the couples would start on opposite feet.

8 COUNT JITTERBUG — For song and dance it is sometimes useful to add two more counts to this JITTERBUG pattern so that it more closely matches the phrases of a song. This is done by adding two walking steps in place on counts 7 and 8. So, the 8 count pattern would be:

Toe heel L (1-2)
Toe heel R (3-4)
Back step L R (5-6)
Step L, Step R (7-8)

For a more athletic JITTERBUG, some dancers may want to change each of the "toe heel" steps to three little steps in place. This would mean:

Step Ball Change (L-R-L)
Step Ball Change (R-L-R)
Back step (L-R)

Again for song and dance you could still add the two more walking steps to make this pattern an 8 instead of a 6 count routine.

STEP KICKS AS PARTNERS — Since you have now mastered step kicks and several partnered dance moves why not try some step kicks with your partner?

For a CHARLESTON type look try holding both hands and facing one another. Hop kick four times on one foot, then four on the other. Then two on each foot and one each for four kicks. If you are both stepping and kicking the same foot it will appear as though you are working in opposition and yet you won't be kicking each other!

Try step kicking toward the front holding your partner in a traditional ballroom dance position for a Jitterbug or Lindy feel.

If the men hold their partner's hands from behind and both kick off to the same side, it gives a feeling of an old-fashioned Cakewalk.

Step kicks - Ballroom dance

Step kicks - Cakewalk

Charleston partnered step kicks

PUTTING IT ALL TOGETHER

Even a novice choreographer, or perhaps especially a novice, is by now realizing that there is an unlimited amount of dance steps and moves to draw from in creating their unique works of art. Having a repertoire of steps to choose from and adapt are the tools by which we exercise our creativity. There is actually very little "right" or "wrong" when you are experimenting with your music and dance. There is no set order that must be followed, no ideas that are fundamentally taboo, no song or dance not worth trying. In many cases, it's up to you to define your style and to push the envelope of what you find exciting and artistically rewarding. However, by now you are also starting to realize that having a working knowledge of the traditional "tools of your trade" will stimulate your creative juices and make you better able to pass your ideas on to your cast and subsequently to your audience.

While there is no "right" or "wrong" way to approach your creative endeavors, isn't it a relief to know that a lot of the work has been done for you? Like music and other art forms, there is a history of dance and staging that has been around long enough to develop a concrete theory of what works and what doesn't. Can you imagine the state of western music if there were actually no rules to guide it? What if there was no framework with in which we were able to be more creative?

Some of the easiest dances to choreograph for the stage are historical and character dances that are taken from our past. In essence, these dances have already been created for you! Your job has become less the designer and more the teacher. All of the dance steps that we have discussed so far can be the jumping-off place for your creations. Putting them together, adapting them to your special tastes and needs is the next "step" to making a bunch of out-of-context-moves into effective dance routines.

In this chapter, we'll begin to put some dances together into longer routines and we'll show how these routines were put to music and utilized in a real performance. These are by no means all of the choices available to you. In fact, this is merely a tip-of-the-iceberg look at what is already available to you even with only a relatively small vocabulary of moves to choose from.

CONTEMPORARY

"Streets Afire" by Mark Brymer (Editor's note: All titles listed in this book refer to musical numbers staged in the accompanying video series video *Step 2 - Putting It All Together*.)

Which of the steps that we have already learned can be modified to be used as an effective contemporary dance? The answer is: "Lots!"

COMBINATION — A combination is a series of dance moves done in succession to make a longer routine.

LINE DANCES — If you put several people in a row (or several rows), all facing the same direction and all do a dance "combination" that is repetitive and performed without a specific partner, you are doing a LINE DANCE. Examples of a LINE DANCE are "The Dip," "The Harlem Shuffle" and "The Achy Breaky."

HUSTLE — "The Hustle" is a line dance combination that has been around for a long time. It utilizes many of the dance steps that we have already learned in the earlier portions of this book.

With your cast (or in the safe privacy of your own dance studio) try this combination of dance steps for a version of THE HUSTLE that is easy, fun and conducive to being able to sing and perform it at the same time.

SECTION (A)

1-4 Walk forward for four even steps beginning with the left foot.

5 Put your left heel forward as you lean back.

6 Put your left foot back as you lean forward.

7 Put your feet together and hands to your sides.

& 8 Turn your toes quickly in and out using the balls of both feet.

9-12 Do a "three point turn" to your left with your hands behind your back until you clap on count 12.

13-16 Do a similar 'Three point turn" to the right clapping on count 16.

SECTION (B)

1-4 Back up four steps again starting with your left foot.

5-8 Repeat counts 5-8 of the previous 16 counts.

9-16 PULL BACKS — Facing left step back (LR) on "and nine" pushing your hips far stage right and throwing both hands far to the left at about waist height.

On beat "10" Pull your hands back to your sides as your hips pull toward stage left. Repeat this move for a total of four times.

SECTION (C)

1-4 Walk back to the left to your original starting position.

&5 Bow and Arrow Step quickly (L R) with the right foot crossing in front of the left. At the same time pull your hands apart at shoulder level as if you are drawing a "Bow and Arrow"

Bow and arrow

6-8 Pull your elbows into your sides and swivel around to the left in one complete rotation.

9-16 REPLACEMENT STEP — Extend your right leg far out to the right with almost all of your weight going to the left foot. Snap your right fingers low and in front and your left fingers behind your back. After two counts replace your left foot with your right so that your left leg is extended far out to the left and the weight is almost entirely onto your right foot. Now your hands have switched so that the left is in front and the right behind. Do this switch four times.

Foot replacement

SECTION (D)

1-16 WINNIE-THE-POOH HIPS — Put your feet in a wide second and sit down into it. Keep your "fistettes" at your hips. Without straightening your legs swing your hips from left to right, back and forth for 16 counts. It reminds one of WINNIE THE POOH dancing, Well, it reminds *me* of WINNIE THE POOH dancing. As long as we all know what it means it doesn't really matter what you call a step!

Winnie the Pooh hips

Try all of the four stages of this HUSTLE dance several times to different music.

If you have the video series that accompanies this book notice how the routine was used in Mark Brymer's selection "Street's Afire!"

Experiment with rearranging the order of the different sections of this HUSTLE routine and see how they can work in a variety of ways.

BODY PERCUSSION

Of course, everybody beyond the age of about eight months knows about "clapping" and how visually exciting, as well as aurally, it can be. But, there are a lot of other "body percussion" moves that can make for exciting sounds and sights on the stage.

STAGE CLAP — Most of the excitement of clapping on stage should be visual more than aural. It needs to "look" exciting without covering up the music to which you are clapping. A STAGE CLAP is achieved by either (1) pulling back just as your hands are about to connect there by letting out a higher and lighter sound, or (2) clapping only the fingers of one hand into the palm of the other so that the sound is less. Of course, there may be times when you want a very loud clap sound. This can be achieved by cupping each hand and clapping them together for a lower, more reverberating result.

SLAPPING THIGHS AND KNEES — Especially appropriate for country dances, is the slapping of your thighs on the off beats. Try it while marching with your knees turned out or just standing still.

Country thigh-slapping

FLOOR PERCUSSION — Besides tap dancing or country clogging, the floor can also be percussion instrument for the hand. Notice the difference in sound you get by slapping the floor as opposed to stamping on it. Try slapping the floor with your right hand on one, clapping on two, hitting both of your thighs with your open hands on three, and clapping again on four for a pattern of sound made interesting by three unique slapping sounds.

8 COUNT CLAP PATTERNS
Here are a couple of exciting eight count patterns of slapping and clapping that are good for both exercises in coordination and concentration, plus make for excellent song and dance routines.

Pattern (A)
1 Clap
2 Slap your right thigh with your right hand.
3 Slap your left thigh with your left hand.
4 Clap
5 Pick up and hit your left heel with your right hand behind yourself.
6 Slap your left thigh with your left hand.
7 Slap your right thigh with your right hand.
8 Clap

Pattern (B)
Stand on your right foot to prepare.
1 Step onto your left foot.
2 Lift and hit your right thigh with both hands.
3 Put your right foot down with the weight still on your left foot.
4 Clap
5 Lift and hit again your right thigh with both hands.
6 Put your right foot down again with your weight still on the left foot.
7 Clap
8 For a third time, lift and hit your right thigh with both hands.

Repeat that entire routine to the opposite side. In other words, step right first and the slaps will be onto the left leg on counts 2,5 and 8. Can you do it faster and faster? This a great routine for a Country dance.

WHACK ATTACK — here's a sixteen count clapping, slapping, whacking pattern that some call a "Major" WHACK ATTACK. It can be a lot of fun for a song like "Fascinatin' Rhythm" or "I Got Rhythm."

1   Clap
2   Slap right leg with right hand.
3   Slap left leg with left hand.
4   Clap
5   Hit left heel with right hand behind your right knee.
6   Slap left leg with left hand.
7   Slap right leg with right hand.
8   Clap
9   Tap right side of your face with right hand.
10   Tap left side of your face with left hand.
11   Slap right leg with right hand.
12   Slap left leg with left hand.
13-16 Clap four times.

Have a good time coming up with variations of the WHACK ATTACK and other body percussion routines. A great exercise that works as an fascinating piece of stage movement is to come up with two, three, four or more patterns and have different groups on stage perform them simultaneously. All of the different sounds of the body, the floor, or the walls make for a human percussion section unmatched by even the finest trap set.

PERSONALITY DANCE STEPS

Many of the world's most memorable performing artists had unique walks, moves or dances that became their trademark and are still recognizable today. Taken literally, or modified to suit your needs, these moves can often be easily communicated to a cast and used in an actual performance.

THE CHARLIE CHAPLIN WALK — Heels together, toes apart. Walk like a penguin. You might even throw in a frog jump once in a while by pulling your heels right up under you as you go straight up in the air. Twirl an umbrella, a watch chain or a walking stick as you go, or just hold onto your Derby.

Charlie Chaplin walk/jump

THE CURLY SHUFFLE — Named after one of the famous THREE STOOGES, the dancers hop backwards in profile to stage left or right, pushing off with the other foot.

The Curly Shuffle

JACKIE GLEASON — "And away we go....!" Wind up and bring your right foot in front of the left before you exit stage right.

The Jackie Gleason

JIMMY DURANTE WALK — Walk stiff legged shaking your hat or upstage hand, leaning forward and shaking your head as you go.

The Jimmy Durante

THE TEABERRY SHUFFLE — This is taken from the old television commercial for Teaberry Gum. It takes four counts:

1 Hop on both feet. Feet apart.
2 Weight on left foot, bring right foot behind the left knee.
3 Hop on both spread feet again.
4 Weight on right foot, bring left foot behind the right knee.

Teaberry 3

Teaberry 1

Teaberry 4

Teaberry 2

THE SOUPY SHUFFLE — Named for the actor/comedian Soupy Sales, this involves sliding from one side to the other while picking up the knee and leading with the hip of the direction you are moving.

The Soupy Shuffle

THE SOFT SHOE

Featuring excerpts from "SRO" arranged by Mark Brymer (From the accompanying Video STEP 2 — PUTTING IT ALL TOGETHER)

Everybody ought to learn how to do a soft shoe. First of all, because it is so much fun to do. Secondly, because it is so easy to do. Thirdly, because it is very useful for stage work as it suits so many song and dance routines. (It is designed specifically for singing and dancing together) And fifth, because can you imagine being able to do a SOFT SHOE and then not doing it?!?

Here is a basic soft shoe routine that can work for lots and lots of songs. Try it to tunes like "Harrigan," "Give Me That Old Soft Shoe," "Tea For Two," "Me And My Shadow," "Carolina In The Morning," "One" (From A CHORUS LINE), "Once In Love With Amy," even "Rudolph The Red-Nosed Reindeer"! How many more songs can you think of that have the feel of a soft shoe?

A basic soft shoe step is just a walking pattern on the floor.

Counts 1-4 — Face downstage left. Step left, right a bit further down left, and then back on the left foot again. Hold for the fourth count.

Counts 5-8 — Face downstage right. Step right, left a bit further down right, and then back on the right foot again. Hold for the fourth count.

Counts 9-16 — Face down stage left. Step left, right a bit further down left, back on the left, right a bit further upstage right, forward on the left, right a bit further down left again, and back to where you began on the left foot.

Repeat those 16 counts now beginning to the right.

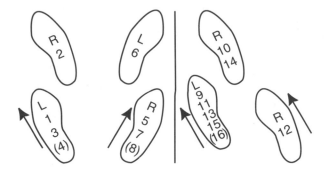
The Soft Shoe

PADDLE WHEEL TURN — Walk seven steps in a dotted pattern turning around yourself to the left, almost as if your left foot is nailed to the floor. Left arm down, right arm up, like a banking airplane. Repeat to the right with switched arms.

Paddle Wheel Turn

Can you see how a paddle wheel turn could be modified to look like a COUNTRY DANCE? CONGA? CHARLESTON?

SWAYS — Swaying is simply a move from one side to the other without going anyplace. Practice different kinds of sways. One of the nicest is to lead with your shoulder.

For a soft shoe sway, try it with somewhat relaxed jazz hands at about shoulder height.

Sway - lead with shoulders

Sway - jazz hands

SOFT SHOE BODY PERCUSSION —
There are a lot of choices of body percussion that would be appropriate for soft shoe. Try one triplet slap on your thighs followed by a quarter note. Then, hit your left heel with your right hand. Follow this with two step kicks. Repeat the pattern a few times.

Now, put some of your new soft shoe moves together for an entire routine. If you have the video version of GOTTA SING GOTTA DANCE STEP 2, watch some young performers use these moves for the song "Harrigan" arranged by Mark Brymer in his revue "SRO"!

COUNTRY

What are the distinguishing characteristics of a basic country dance? There are many. But, some that are universally-recognized, and good to have in your creative cache, are (a) Knees turned out like you've been riding a horse for a long time (b) Consistent use of fists (c) Prominent use of elbows (d) Slapping your thighs or clapping on the off beats (e) Flexed feet.

Here's a short routine of country-style steps that you might be able to incorporate verbatim into your next country song and dance, or modify to suit your needs.

"Next To Lovin' I Like Fightin'"
Arranged by Kirby Shaw
(Featured on GOTTA SING, GOTTA DANCE Video Step 2)

Counts 1-4   Soupy Shuffle — Do the Soupy Shuffle four times alternating R L R L and backing up as you do them.

Counts 5-7   Walk stiff legged (kicking those straight legs out to the side.) toward the audience L R L.

Straight-leg walk

& 8   One frog jump lifting your heels up beneath you as you jump straight up.

Frog jump

1-4 Face down stage left. Step L and drag your right foot along behind until it catches up with the left. Do this four times very quickly while cranking your fully extended right arm underhanded as if you were winding up for a punch.

Fist crank

5-8 Curly Shuffle four times moving backward and upstage right to get back to where you started.

Curly Shuffle

Try to create some other routines using the vocabulary of moves that you now have. Do you see how you can modify almost any step you can think of to make it look country? Try to do a country PADDLE WHEEL TURN. How about a COUNTRY GRAPEVINE? Try some BODY PERCUSSION in a country style. How about STEP KICKS? BOX STEPS? or even just MARCHING?

DANCES OF THE 1950s

"We Go Together" (from GREASE) Arranged by Ed Lojeski (Featured on GOTTA SING, GOTTA DANCE Video Step 2)

Of course, every period of music has a wide array of wonderful dances to accompany the era. Some of the most popular, and still recent enough to remember are the dances of the 1950s. Here are a few of the favorites of that era that are easy to adapt to stage song and dance.

TOE HEEL/TOE HEEL
Put all of your weight onto your right foot and put your snapping fingers over your head. Now twist your left foot while hopping on the right. The pattern is
1 toe
2 heel
3 toe
4 heel

Then hop onto the left foot for four counts as the right foot twists;
5 toe
6 heel
7 toe
8 heel

Repeat this for another eight counts or repeat it but switch sides every two counts instead of every four.

THE TWIST — This is the dance made famous by Chubby Checker. Naturally it would be very effective simply twisting back and forth like you've seen on TV. However, there are ways to make even the twist more uniform and perhaps more interesting to watch. Face directly toward the audience and try this eight count twist pattern.

1 Lift your left knee across the front as your arms counter in the opposite direction.
2-3 Twist hips and arms in opposition. Arms are now going R L.
4 Lift your right knee across the front as the hands go right.
5-6 Twist two more times.
7 Lift your left knee again across the front the same as beat 1.
8 Put left leg back over to the left but don't put any weight on it.

The arms in this routine are actually just swinging across the front (L R L R L R L R) for all eight counts, working in opposition with the twisting and lifting legs and hips.

Twist - beat 1 & 7

Twist - beat 4

RIB CAGE ISOLATIONS — An "isolation" literally means that the rib cage is all that is moving during this move. But, in this 1950s rib cage isolation we will add the use of your legs and arms to amplify what the rib cage is doing.

Bend your knees slightly and turn them in towards each other. Begin with your jazz hands at chest level, palms in, elbows up.

1   Put your right heel out to the side and open up your arms.
2   Return to the beginning position.
3   Put your left heel out to the left and open your arms again.
4   Return to starting position.
5-6   Repeat 1 and 2.
7-8   Repeat one and two again.

So the pattern for the first eight counts is
1 (R) - 3 (L) - 5 (R) - 7 (R)

For the next pattern of eight it would begin Left and be just the opposite.
1 (L) - 3 (R) - 5 (L) — 7 (L)

Rib cage isolation - out

Rib cage isolation - in

HAND JIVE — Unless you have been living under a rock for the last thirty years you already know what HAND JIVE is, and hopefully you already realize that it can be a lot of fun as an accompanying move on stage for just about any rock 'n roll song of the 1950s. It is especially good if you are in very limited space or if you have a large cast and want to have some layering effects going on. A few jitterbugging couples backed up by a chorus full of "HAND JIVERS" can make for a very entertaining picture!

The classic HAND JIVE takes up sixteen counts and is a series of hand claps and an assortment of related moves. One version goes like this:

1-2	Hit your thighs two times.
3-4	Clap twice
5-6	Wipe blade hands over each other twice, left over right.
7-8	Wipe blade hands over each other twice, right over left.
9-10	Pound fists on top of each other twice, left over right.
11-12	Pound fists on top of each other twice, right over left.
13-14	Throw right thumb over right shoulder like a baseball umpire calling an "out!" two times.
15-16	Similarly, throw the left thumb over the left shoulder two times.

Repeat the whole process over and over until you can't stand it any longer, or until the song is over.

THE MASHED POTATO — Put your hands in your arm pits. Keep your knees together and smash your R foot down as you flop your elbows down on the first beat. Lift that same R foot up and smash it down again on beats 3, 5, and 7. Do the same with the left foot for eight counts or four smashes. Then do two on the right for four counts and two on the left for four counts. Lastly, do one R then L then R then L for eight more counts. Do you recognize the familiar pattern of 4 - 4, 2 - 2, 1 - 1 - 1 - 1?

The Mashed Potato

THE FREDDIE — "The Freddie" is a very athletic dance that bears a striking resemblance to the calisthenics we all know as the "JUMPING JACK." The only real difference is that when both of your hands are meeting at the top, one foot is straight out to the side. Alternating legs should be up on 1, 3, 5, 7, and down to the floor on 2, 4, 6, 8. This can be a very funny dance to do individually or as an entire group and works well for the wild dances of the 1950's and even into the '60s.

The Freddie

THE JERK — To do THE JERK, plant your feet about shoulder width apart facing downstage right. At the same time, put your right hand over your head with a 90 degree bent elbow. The left hand is low and back in a similar 90 degree bent position. The fingers of both hands are ready to be "snapped." In this position, the chest is extended downstage right and the back is arched. On the next count, the arms are thrown forward, the fingers are snapped and the chest is contracted so that the back becomes rounded.

Next, try the exact same move to the opposite corner with the left arm up and the right back, etc.

The Jerk - 1

The Jerk - 2

The Swim - 1

The Swim - 3

THE SWIM — Well, guess what this dance looks like! Actually, there are several variations of THE SWIM. Basically, you can do THE AMERICAN CRAWL, THE BREAST STROKE, THE BACK STROKE or "GOING UNDER FOR THE LAST TIME." Besides the variations you can incorporate from the waist up, try a couple of different feet positions.

• Put your feet in a wide, parallel "second" position. Alternately, bend your knees as fast as you can to get a "shimmying" effect. This is usually the best choice for male dancers that are doing THE SWIM.

• You could choose to put your feet together, perhaps with one knee bent slightly in front of the other like an "S POSE." In this more "feminine" position you could "bop" one hip as you SWIM.

The Swim - 2

The Swim - 4

THE PONY — This dance consists of three steps, hopping from one foot to the other but staying essentially in one place. The beats and their accompanying steps involve two PONIES per measure, one to the left and one to the right:

```
L   R   L   R   L   R
1   &   2   3   &   4
```

There are several choices for what to do with your arms and hands.
- The easiest is simply to put your hands on your hips in open or "fist" position.
- You can get your hands out of the picture by putting them behind your back.
- Put one hand on your hip and swing the other over your head as though you are swinging a lasso.
- On alternating "Ponies" put your wrists together overhead when stepping left on "one and two" and flexed at you sides on beats "Three and four" as you PONY to the right.
- Do THE PONY and THE HAND JIVE at the same time.

The Pony - 1

The Pony - 3

The Pony - 2

The Pony - 4

Can you think of songs where the Pony, the Jerk, the Freddie, the Mashed Potato, Hand Jive, and the Twist will all work?

How about "It's My Party," "Twist and Shout," "Hound Dog," "Blue Suede Shoes," "Rock and Roll Is Here To Stay," "Shake, Rattle, and Roll" or almost any song ever recorded by THE BEACH BOYS!

FORMATIONS

Dance is a great way to express music, enhance the message of your lyrics and make your song-and-dance performances more interesting and entertaining for your audience. Before or beyond dance steps, however, there are a lot of choices you can make about how you arrange your cast on stage. Very often these "staging" choices will not affect the quality of the sound your cast is making but will greatly enhance the visual end of your "live" performance. Sometimes a change in staging position will actually help the quality of the music that you are performing since the same voice parts can be grouped together, or separated, soloists and small groups can be highlighted, and the dynamics of your concert show order can be reflected visually.

TRAFFIC — Traffic means the movement of your cast on stage from one position to another. It does not necessarily refer to the dance steps or moves that you use to get to this new position but just the action itself. Sometimes just the visual effect of an entire cast moving from one formation to the other can be visually interesting enough to make a number very effective. TRAFFIC can also refer to the movement of the cast between selections.

So, putting aside our interest in dance for a moment let's consider some of the basic stage formations that can be put to use by even the most traditional choirs. These formations can serve as a way to make any performance more visually stimulating, whether the choir is moving or standing still.

DIAMONDS — The cast simply stands in a DIAMOND formation. However, experiment with variations on this basic DIAMOND formation. For instance, try one DIAMOND inside of the other. Try three or four inside of each other depending on the size of your cast. How about side by side DIAMONDS or many on stage at once.

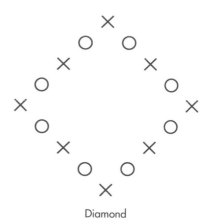

Diamond

"V" FORMATIONS — This means forming a V on stage, single, double, convex or concave. Try one inside of the other, or several. Experiment with making the "point" of the "V" in different places and with different angles on stage.

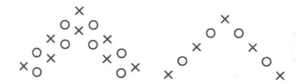

Double "V" Formation

"V" Formation

DIAGONALS — Single, double, triple lines of cast members on stage. They can intersect, relate obliquely, make a perfect "X" or one of any number of choices.

their right put the altos in a reverse BOWLING PIN FORMATION and the sopranos to their left, also in reverse. Now you have a block of people but the visual to the audience is also of three BOWLING PIN pyramids.

Three bowling pins

2 diagonals, 3 diagonals, and "X"

Diagonal lines

Bowling pin - single

BOWLING PIN — This is a pyramid of people starting with one in the front, two behind that person, then three, four, five and so on like bowling pins in an alley. This is a great formation on stage for keeping everybody at least partially visible. It is also good for a cast of varying abilities. If you have one very good performer that you want your entire group to reflect, put him or her at the front of your BOWLING PIN formation. The audience's eyes are immediately drawn to that front and center performer and it can appear as though the entire group is as polished and effective as that one.

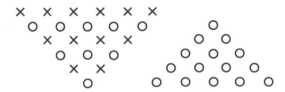

Bowling pin and reverse bowling pin

Bowling pin - reversed

Like the V FORMATION, try the BOWLING PIN FORMATION in reverse. Try two or three on stage at once, either separated or in a block. For instance, put the men in the middle in a BOWLING PIN FORMATION. To

Bowling pin - change of focus

FAMILY PORTRAIT — This features the cast standing in a formation as if they were having their picture taken. As with a real photo session, the most important thing is that everybody can be seen. Some can kneel, sit, crouch, or stand.

Family Portrait

With all of the many different formations you can come up with on the stage, each of them can be given a totally new look if the focus of your group is modified. For instance, have your cast stand in any one of the above formations facing directly down-stage, the BOWLING PIN FORMATION, for example. For the second number or verse, have the cast turn to face downstage left. Even the director can stand down left. For the third number, have the cast face downstage right and have the front person step out to sing a solo. For the fourth selection adjust your

BOWLING PIN formation into a FAMILY PORTRAIT for a new look without having to change any body's location on stage.

This sort of variety can be utilized in any of your cast formations. We'll examine more when we talk about staging the concert performance.

STRENGTHS OF THE STAGE

Through years of experience, experts in staging and directing live productions have discovered that there are actually places and positions on the stage that will emotionally strike an audience in predictable ways. Much like "body language" there is an emotional language to the areas of the stage of which any effective choreographer or stage director must be aware.

The strongest area of the stage is DOWNSTAGE RIGHT. Possibly because of the way westerners read, when an audience hears a sound and wants to see where it comes from, they will begin with the area of the stage to their left (DOWNSTAGE RIGHT) and scan the stage much like they read a book. This is very important for a director to know, especially if the goal is to present a strong and confident message.

The next strongest area is DOWNSTAGE CENTER.

Following this theory, the weakest place on the stage would be UPSTAGE LEFT. In the reading-like approach your audience takes to watching the stage, this will be the last place their eyes will come to rest. If you have a soloist that you want to appear vulnerable or distant the place to stage them begins at UPSTAGE LEFT.

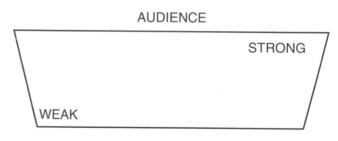
Strong and weak stage areas

Of course, there are always exceptions to every rule and creative people will never want to be tied down. Still, these are valuable tools to have at your disposal as you examine your work and try to make it more effective, and to make it more efficiently reflect the message of your art.

59

TRANSITIONS — One of the places that a choreographer and/or stage director can make a big difference in a show or concert is in their attention to the transitions between songs, numbers and acts. This is where real creativity can occur without affecting the individual numbers themselves. It is one of the detail areas that will really reflect the care that an ensemble has for every element of the show. You can use this time to thank the audience for their response to your last number or set up the next. It can be a place to introduce the individual personalities of the cast, and create "moments" that the audience will remember long after the final curtain descends. Of course, there are unlimited methods for creating effective transitions.

There is the Master of Ceremonies approach, where an individual cast member simply introduces what is going to happen next, or acknowledges the performers of the last show element. This is the Ed Sullivan approach which tends to be quite formal and not necessarily the most interesting. However, it can give a legitimate sense of continuity to a performance which will leave an audience feeling comfortable and friendly.

A second choice would be to use different members of the cast to introduce each number. This gives the audience an opportunity to become better acquainted with the individual people in the production. An audience generally enjoys getting to know the people on stage.

Try to think of ways that you can keep your production moving along. Is it really necessary to introduce each song? If the first line of the song is setting up the mood or story line, do you really have to explain it first to

your audience? How often can you make a direct segue without pausing for an explanatory introduction?

Use an appropriate piece of poetry delivered by one of the cast members to make the transition an artistic part of the show.

Try to make your transition musical. On occasion:
- Use another chorus of the former song to make the change of position you have chosen that gets you ready for the next selection.
- Jump directly into the musical introduction of the new song and use it to change your formation.
- Use a completely different song, or at least a portion of a song, in between two features to make the transition physically and to set the scene for the next act. For instance, an instrumental chorus of "Let Me Call You Sweetheart" might make an appropriate transition into "My Funny Valentine" or "A Bicycle Built For Two." A simple chorus of "You're A Grand Old Flag" would be a great introduction to "God Bless America" or "America The Beautiful." How about a female soloist performing a portion of Gerswin's "Summertime" as a great transition into "In The Good Old Summertime" or a collection of southern spirituals.
- Reprise a portion of the song that you have just finished as a suitable transition.

Transitions are simply sensitive programming and pacing of your concert. Eleven madrigals in a row can even make such fun music tedious. An entire evening of country western ballads can be downright depressing. If variety is indeed the

spice of life, there is no place better to demonstrate it than in the pacing of your show, and one of the best areas to add variety is in your transitions.

Another important reminder about transitions (musical and/or staging) is that, like any element of your performance, transitions MUST be rehearsed and perfected. Just because one song is completed does not mean that the audience has somehow disappeared for the few seconds it takes you to get to the next element. The next element IS the TRANSITION. We have all been in the audience of the musical that is high in quality except for the excruciatingly long time in between one act and the next. Each and every one of these moments should be well rehearsed, critiqued and modified so that you are certain that it is sending the exact message that you wish to convey to your audience. Some directors will even use a stop watch and challenge their cast members to "beat the clock" in moving sets or bodies on stage. It is not necessarily the case that every transition be "short," but it is necessary that it be interesting, or at least not negatively effective to your guests.

These are the kinds of details that will make your performance go from being average to being exceptional. Audiences are very aware of a cast that has appreciated them enough to pay attention to the elements that may initially seem small on the list of priorities. An audience likes to feel that you value their time and attention. They should not have to tolerate "dead" time, or throw-away moments from the stage.

STAGING YOUR TRANSITIONS — The staging director can do a lot to make the transitions interesting and smooth, (not to mention quick and appropriate!). Here are some questions to ask yourself as you begin to design your transitions:

- Is the movement aiding in the setting of the mood for the upcoming scene? (For example: You have just finished a rousing dance number and are moving into a ballad. Which would help you set the mood for the next songs emotion? A reprise of the dance number? The quiet introduction of the upcoming ballad? A piece of poetry? An introduction by a Master of Ceremonies?) Keep in mind that there are usually no absolutely right or wrong answers to situations like this. Your job is to ask the questions of yourself, experiment with the different possibilities, and decide on what you feel is the most effective.

- Are the cast members having to move long distances to get to their starting positions for the next number? If so, is there a way that they can change their starting positions? Is there a more interesting way that they could get to their new positions?

- Is the transition taking so long that it is uncomfortable for your audience? These people did not leave the relative comfort of their homes to witness your insensitivity. You must make it pleasant, or at least not annoying, for them. They are your guests. Consider how they feel. If you want them to feel uncomfortable, that is your choice. But, at least be aware that you are doing so.

TAGS — This refers to a piece of music, a bit of staging, or both, that follows a full piece of music. For example, it may be the last two bars of music that ended the song, or it may be the refrain repeated one more time for bows or a move to the next song. One of the most famous

"TAGS" is the old "Shave and a Haircut" routine at the end of a tap dance, country or clogging routine.

LIFTS

LIFTS are, at the same time, fun to do, terrific audience pleasers, and frighteningly dangerous if not properly supervised, taught and rehearsed. Safety of both the "lifter" and the "liftee" is of the utmost importance. Lifts should never be attempted without proper supervision by someone who understands how the lift is supposed to work, where the danger spots of the process are, and how to "spot" the participants to make certain that no one will get hurt. No amount of audience appeal is worth injuring a performer.

A frequent misconception is that the work involved in a lift is left up to the "lifter" with the "liftee" simply along for the ride. In truth, much (if not most) of the labor is properly left up to the one being lifted. Their understanding and execution of the principles of leverage are crucial in the proper execution of any lift. It is a shared effort.

There are many styles of music where LIFTS are appropriate. Music of the Jitterbug, Charleston and Disco eras are all inclusive of opportunities to add lifts to your routines. They can also be used in Country Dance, Caribbean and African dance as well as most other ethnic or period styles dating way back to the original waltz and even the Tango.

Here are a few of the more well known lifts that you might recognize and may even wish to try with your performers under the proper supervision of someone who is trained for such activities. This might very well include the physical education teacher or a gymnastic coach in your school.

BABY CARRIAGE — Notice how the girl's arm is around the lifter's shoulder's in a way as to not put too much pressure on his neck. Improper pressure on that area of the spine could cause serious injury. Notice that the girl's feet are pointed, although a flexed foot would give more of a country feel. Experiment with different variations of this lift such as one pointed leg and one bent, both legs straight, one arm extended or both arms around the lifter's neck.

Baby Carriage lift - 1

Baby Carriage lift - 2

SHIN LIFT — This can be a fun and effective pose for a 1920s style dance or even a country routine.

Shin lift

STRADDLE POSITION — Try spinning around in this position in either a country style or for a jitterbug routine. The person who is being lifted can help a great deal by holding up her own weight with her forearms on the front of her lifter. Again, the "lifted" should be careful not to put the weight on the back of the "lifter's" neck.

Straddle position

CHEEK TO CHEEK — Notice which "cheeks" are together. There is another "CHEEK TO CHEEK" that doesn't entail any lifting that I'll leave to you to figure out! With this lift, be very careful because there can be a tendency for the lifted's momentum to carry her right over the top of her partner. Again make sure you have plenty of capable spotters. This lift can be approached either from the floor or from a straddle position. Make sure that you both know whether or not you are going to return to the floor or to the straddle before you start the lift!

Cheek to cheek

HIP LIFT, LEGS TO THE CEILING —
This is a relatively simple lift with only a
couple of fundamental concerns of
which to be aware. Notice how the
"lifted's" hands can either be clasped
behind the neck of the "lifter" or can be
held in a traditional "ball room dance
position" which offers a lot of stability
and leverage. See how the "lifter's" feet
are far enough apart and knees bent
enough to offer a ledge for the small of
the back of the one he is lifting to rest
upon. In this way, all of the weight is
not supported by the strength of your
arms and you are actually balancing
the "liftee" as opposed to holding her
up. Make sure the "lifted" is far enough
so that her feet are pointing straight up
to the ceiling. Anything less than this
can make for a lot of extra work and
for a less impressive lift.

Try the lift to either side setting the
lifted on the floor in between.
Can you try the lift to both sides with
no stop at the floor in between? Make
sure that both the lifter and the liftee
know before hand which version they
are about to attempt.

THE WRAP AROUND — This is quite a
difficult lift that requires precise timing
and physical effort on the part of both
participants. It begins and ends with a
BABY CARRIAGE LIFT with the lifter
wrapping the liftee around his body in
one complete revolution. Although the lift
should be completed in one continuous
motion so that the momentum of the
swing can aid in the "wrapping," it
should be rehearsed one step at a time.
First, lift the girl into a baby carriage lift.
Wind up and swing her legs around at
the waist level. The lifter then grabs the
liftee's legs above the knees and the liftee
bends the knees so that the lifter and the
liftee are locked together. Then, let go of
the lifter's neck as the lifter swings the
upper body of the liftee around and
back to the Baby Carriage lift. As the
liftee is coming back to the front it will
require considerable use of their stomach
muscles to help pull up to the original
sitting position. This is not an easy lift
and as always should be closely
supervised whenever attempted.

Wrap around - 2

Wrap around - 3

Wrap around - 1

PULL THROUGH — Here are two versions
of the pull-through-the-legs lift that is
popular when choreographing songs of
the '20s through '70s and beyond. The
difference is simply whether or not you
cross your hands before you attempt the
rest of the maneuver or not. This will effect
which way the "pulled" person ends up
facing at the completion of the lift.

Hip lift, legs to the ceiling

- Step one is to hold hands with while facing your partner. If one of you crosses your arms at this time you should end up facing away from your partner at the lift's completion. If neither of you cross your arms here it will be easier to wind up facing each other at the lift's end.
- Step two is for the liftee to squat down or at least duck.
- Step three is for the lifter to swing one leg over the head of his partner so that he is facing away from that person and still continuing to hold hands.
- Step four is for the liftee to slide through the legs of the lifter, feet first.
- As this slide is complete the lifter should pull straight up on the hands of the liftee to pull them back to their feet. During this time the liftee either does a half twist to wind up facing the lifter or does no twist and winds up facing away from the lifter.

Pull-through - 2

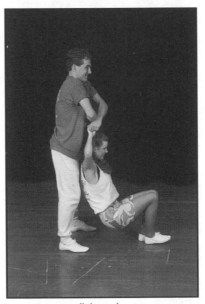
Pull through - 3

Pull-through - 1

HIP LIFT — Here's a great lift to end a song or even for the middle a routine since it is quite quick to get "in and out of." Like most lifts there is an equal amount of exertion needed from both participants. The girl's inside arm carries most of the weight of the lift by pressing onto the shoulders of the lifter. The lifter's inside arm is there mostly for balance and minor lifting responsibility. Make sure that you are high enough on the hip that you have an added ledge for the lifted to settle on.

Hip lift

PIGGY BACK LIFT — Notice that on this great country style lift that the lifter can use his hands on his thighs with locked arms to take some of the pressure off his back. In this lift, the bottom person becomes essentially a tripod. They can't help a lot with the lift itself except to provide a sturdy base from which the liftee can perch. The liftee has the responsibility of making sure that the lifter is set and stable before they "make the leap" onto his back.

Piggy back lift

SHOULDER LIFT — A shoulder lift can be accomplished with one or two lifters and a liftee.

With a single lifter the liftee should stand in front of and slightly to one side of the lifter, both participants are facing down stage. The lifter puts his hands on her waist being careful not to "dig-in" with his thumbs or any other finger. The liftee should hold onto the wrists of the lifter. This will be your primary leverage point as you execute the lift. One of the most important facets of this particular lift is timing. The lifter and the liftee should both plié at the same time. Then the liftee hops straight up as if she was

going to have to hop up onto her partner's shoulder unassisted. Although the lifter can help a little with lift, his primary responsibility ought to be to guide the jumper, balance her when she lands on her shoulder, and stabilize her when she settles there. The liftee can help the stabilization by wrapping her legs around her partner's sides once she is on his shoulders.

There are several danger points to be aware of when you are attempting this lift. You must be careful that the liftee doesn't over shoot her goal and fall off the back of the lifter. During rehearsal there should absolutely be a spotter there just in case. Then, when the lifter is setting her down he must make absolutely certain that her feet are solidly on the floor before he lets go of her waist. If all of the safety precautions are in place this can be a very impressive lift, especially for the final pose of a dance routine.

Shoulder lift preparation

Shoulder lift

For a two-person shoulder lift, the lifters will share the burden of lift and balance. They should scoop the lifted up with their shoulders while holding on to the lifted's respective shins. It will help a great deal if the height of the two lifters' shoulders are at about the same level. This is a relatively easy lift as three people are sharing the burden. In some ways it is more impressive to the audience in that three people present a larger picture, and a picture that is symmetrically in tune.

Three-person shoulder lift

TWO-PERSON CART WHEEL — A two-person cartwheel involves one person doing a cartwheel using the lifter's legs as a guide and stabilizing point, and having the lifter guide the cartwheeler throughout the process of the cartwheel by placing their hands on that persons waist. Notice how far apart and secure the lifter's legs are through out the maneuver. This is so that they are not thrown off balance from the added weight and direction of the cartwheeler.

Two-person cartwheel

PRETZEL MOVE — This maneuver is not so much a lift as it is a full routine involving two people holding hands throughout. It is seen most in songs of the 1920s and '30s, and at some quirky fraternity parties!

There are four steps to the move after you have already faced your partner and grabbed hands. These hands will be held throughout.

• First, simultaneously the girl squats as the man swings his RIGHT leg over her head and to the floor. The partners are now face to backside, so don't stay there for very long!

Pretzel - step 1

• Second, the man squats as far as he can as the girl swings her left leg over his head. Keep in mind that you are holding hands through out. Now the two partners will find themselves cheek to cheek in an almost compromising position!

Pretzel - step 2

• Now, moving backwards, the man kicks his left leg over his partner's head making the final position thus far front to back.

Pretzel - step 3

• Finally, the girl kicks her right leg over her squatting partner's head and we are back to where we originally began.

Pretzel - step 4

Try the pretzel using a full eight counts, with two counts for each swing of a leg. This can be a very fun move and a great audience-pleaser. However, don't expect to do much singing while you execute it!

BACK FLIPS — There are a lot of different versions of a back flip using more than one person.

One version is to get into a BABY CARRIAGE lift and then have the lifter simply throw the lifted's legs over her head and help her to land on her feet. This can be very exciting on its own, following a WRAP AROUND, or any other lift that finds you ending in a BABY CARRIAGE position.

Back flip - 1

Back flip - 2

Another possibility is to have the liftee approach the lifter from the right with her left arm upheld. The lifter grabs that wrist with his right hand, puts his left arm under her waist and throws her over as she kicks and tucks.

1-armed assisted back flip

Very similar, and easier for some people, is for the lifter simply to wrap both arms around his partner and flip her as she kicks. Again, make certain that the lifted has both feet on the floor before the lifter lets go of her.

2-armed assisted back flip

OVER-THE-BACK FLIP — Another fun back flip involves the lifter holding both hands or wrists of his partner while facing her. Then they both turn under so that they are back to back. Finally the girl tucks her legs and pulls herself over the rounded back of her partner. He in turn resists her pull for leverage and holds her hands until she is safely over his back with feet on the floor.

Over-the-back flip - 1

Over-the-back flip - 2

Over-the-back flip - 3

Over-the-back flip - 4

There are an unlimited number of creative lifts and creative variations of lifts. But a director or choreographer cannot stress enough the importance of planning, supervision and thoughtful analysis that will protect your performers. Safety is the most important rule!

BOWS

One of the most important, yet often neglected parts of your performance is your bows. This is the last impression that your audience has of you after each number and after each show. This does not mean that every song requires a grand or even small bow, but, acknowledging and thanking your audience for their kindness and support is very important and always appreciated. It, like any other facet of your performance, must be analyzed and rehearsed.

For a youthful and energetic looking bow, try reléve-ing (rising up on your toes) before you actually bow down to your audience. Rise up again onto your toes as you come up from the bow. In terms of counts in a measure you might consider this bow as such:

- Beats 1-3, stand tall with feet together.
- Beat 4, reléve up on your toes.
- On beats 5-6 bend at your waist as far forward as you can letting your arms droop naturally down.
- On beat 7, stand up to releve again.
- On beat 8, lower down to your heels and to your starting position.

Of course, this "UP DOWN UP DOWN" bow can be executed at any tempo, usually relative to the last number you have performed in the program. It is a good idea to practice it at different speeds both to "clean"it up and to examine which speed will be most appropriate in any given situation.

THE GRAND BOW — This much more formal, and usually slower, bow involves lifting your chin on beat one, bowing slowly for three counts and taking the last four counts to come back to a standing position. There is no reléve involved in this bow.

Grand bow - 1

Grand bow - 2

HEAD BOW — This is a more gentle acknowledgment of your audience, often more suitable for more mature performers in more traditional settings. Simply a nod of your head with little or no bend of the waist is often sufficient acknowledgment.

Head bow

CURTSY — This very feminine acknowledgment involves putting one foot behind yourself and bending your knees to a degree that seems suitable to the occasion.

Curtsy - 1

Curtsy - 2

THE COURTIER BOW — Very formal. Feet together. One hand is wrapped around your waist the other behind your back as you bend at the waist. As in all bows, it is appropriate and sensible to remove your hat when you perform a COURTIER BOW.

The one unifying characteristic of all the bows is that your feet should be absolutely together. Feet even a couple of inches apart are a very fast way to reveal an unpolished performance.

Correct bow

Incorrect bow

STAGING THE CONCERT PERFORMANCE

Someone very intelligent once said that "variety is the spice of life." They knew what they were talking about, especially in regard to entertainment, but also in most artistic endeavors. We need to be able to incorporate all kinds of staging into a single performance to add the elements of surprise and contour to our concerts and shows.

We're all used to having special staging and "glitz" for one sort of choral performance and simple, straight-ahead staging for the traditional concert performances. It is at times exciting to consider and encourage visual, as well as musical variety in ALL of our choral performances.

It is exciting to combine avante garde, jazz, top 40, traditional madrigals or all the other different styles of music available on the same program. All you need to do to incorporate the visual aspect to these endeavors is to make a few simple physical changes in your priorities to make your concerts more entertaining and rewarding.

YOU MUST ALWAYS STAGE

This suggestion to make your performances more visually stimulating means that you do not necessarily have to dance to add movement and life to your work . But, you must always give attention to the staging of your work if you agree that you are a part of a visual as well as an audio art. Maybe you have decided that the most effective way to present your music is in four evenly spaced rows of choristers. Fine. You may be right! But, be aware that even that decision was a staging choice that you made. Not a very creative one, but none-the-less legitimate. You can not escape being a staging director if you are asking an audience to look at you as well as listen to you. Recordings, CDs, cassettes and the radio do not need to be staged. Live performances do!

TRADITIONAL CONCERT FORMATION — Of course, there are many ways to stand when on risers and looking at a conductor for the entire musical element. However if you want to perform with a clean and flattering posture that will make your choir appear disciplined and focused, try having them stand with their shoulders turned slightly in toward the conductor, feet together but

with their outside foot slightly forward and pointing directly at the conductor. This will make a clean line without presenting an affected posture. This stance is much easier to make uniform than a stance that has the outside foot further back.

Traditional concert - open

Traditional concert - closed

The encouraging thing abut this traditional block formation is that there are a lot of directions a director can go from this elementary beginning that will make your visual presentation varied and exciting.

• After a song using a two- or four-row block formation, have every other person step forward so that you suddenly have a total of four or eight rows of singers. You will discover that this move does not detract from your musical sound at all but adds a totally new visual point of interest for your audience.The singers in the second, fourth, sixth and eighth rows are said to be standing in the "WINDOWS" of the rows in front of them.

Two rows

Four rows

• After a song or two of this doubled row formation, try a song where all of the singers simply turn at a slight angle to face either down stage left or right. See what a huge difference this variation on focal points makes from an audiences point of view! Even in a traditional "conducted" piece this small change can be very effective.

Block formation facing downstage left

• BOWLING PIN FORMATION — This is obviously a group formation of humans standing like a formation of "bowling pins" or a pyramid. The front row is made up of only one person, the second row has two, then three, four, and so on.

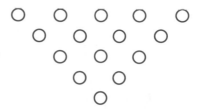

Bowling pin formation - 1

As another variation try making the front of your Bowling Pin formation somewhere other than front and center.

Bowling pin - 2

Try several pyramids or bowling pin formations on the stage at the same time, perhaps one for each voice part will suit your visual and vocal concerns.

See what happens when you make the "point " of your bowling pin formation far upstage.

Bowling pin - 3

Try a several BOWLING PIN FORMATIONS with the "point" alternating between the front and the back.

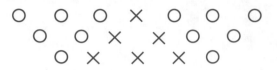
Bowling pin - 4

• DIAGONAL LINES.— This simple variation of diagonal lines is easy to form and very interesting to look at on stage.

Diagonal lines - 1

Diagonal lines - 2

Again, experiment with changes of visual focus and body angles while remaining in your diagonal line formations.

• HALF CIRCLES — Lining up your choir in one, or a series, of half circles, is again interesting and accessible. Like your "BLOCK FORMATION," try doubling your half circles after a song or two by having every other person simply step forward.

Half circles - 1

Half circles - 2

Experiment with changes in focus with your half circles.

SHOULDER-TO-SHOULDER HALF CIRCLES — In other words, the performers are facing into the center of the half circle making the conductor, or at least downstage center the focal point .

Half circles - 3

HALF CIRCLES FACING DIRECTLY FORWARD — Notice how the audience is now the focal point of the group. Notice as well, how even just this slight change of body angle and perhaps focal point change the entire "look and feel" of the staging presentation.

Half circles - 4

FULL CIRCLES — It is an easy maneuver to move your cast from two or more half circles into a full circle. What an interesting change it can be for your audience! Sometimes this kind of a move can be accomplished with great success even within the verses and refrains of one song. Try it, for instance, in a song like AMERICA THE BEAUTIFUL! Perform the first verse and chorus in two concave half circles. Then, use the second verse to move the front lines into a convex half circle that serves to complete a full circle. Try to be there in time for the second chorus and you'll have an appropriate look for the message of "brotherhood" in the middle of the second chorus. Can you think of other songs where a unified circle could better help you convey the message of your music to your audience?

Full circles

Notice how the full circle gives a three dimensional look when the back half is elevated onto a riser.

Refer to the following songs on the accompanying video: STEP 3 - STAGING THE CONCERT PERFORMANCE for an example of the above techniques.

"God Bless The U.S.A."
Arranged by Mark Brymer
"Candle On The Water"
Arranged by Ed Lojeski

An easy way to bring some new faces to the front of your choir is to let your circle rotate during an interlude or even a choral section that won't suffer from the movement and change of focus.

Walking in a circle

NATURE'S ELEVATORS — This is a choreographer's term for a human being's knees. They are called "nature's elevators" because they are the most readily-available tool for creating levels on stage. Adding the dimensions that the knees have to offer gives your staging pictures variations in heights along with the many possibilities of width and depth.

FAMILY PORTRAIT — This refers to a clump of people on stage placed in varying heights, widths and depths so that all faces can be seen, much like a pose you would try to manage when having a "Kodak Moment." There are unlimited variations of this theme depending on the size of the group and how tightly knit you want your family picture to be.

Family portrait - closed

Family portrait - open

See the staging of "Shenandoah" from the choral revue ALL AMERICAN arranged by Mark Brymer on the accompanying video STEP 3 — STAGING THE CONCERT PERFORMANCE.

Don't forget to experiment with different angles and degrees of focus within the realm of a family portrait.

CHORALOGRAPHY

This is a term that is often applied to movement by a traditional choir that falls somewhat short of full-scale dance. It usually implies the use of moves that can be performed in a traditional concert setting that help to dramatize either the lyric or the musical line of the music. In truth, choralography can very often help a choir to sing a work much more musically than if they simply stand in a rigid choral formation. In choralography, the choir uses gestures to interpret the words and music and to help heighten its impact without necessarily launching into full-scale dance. It might be stated that "choralography" is dance executed from the waist up, but as soon as you assert this there will be exceptions that break the rule.

There are certain gestures that through historical trial and error have been determined to project a particular thought, mood, or idea. As a choreographer or choralographer, it is useful to have at your beck and call a working vocabulary of these moves to draw from when you are designing your setting. Here are but a handful of such moves that are universally-recognized as body language that sends a specific, or on occasion, general message to your audience.

Indeed, you may find that these moves will actually make your cast perform more musically as opposed to sacrificing any sense of the musical priority!

SINGLE FISTS — Power, strength, force, conviction, drive, determination, yes!, rock (as in rock 'n' roll), catch, hold, pull, country, unity., etc.

Single fists - 1

Single fists - 2

CLASPED FISTS — Praise, pray, God, unity, togetherness, friendship, higher power, power, etc.

Clasped fists - 1

Clasped fists - 2

FISTS ACROSS CHEST — Bondage, prison, death, captivity, slavery, humbleness, self, bring in, etc.

Crossed fists over chest

Refer to the musical example "Chester" from AMERICAN PORTRAIT arranged by Ed Lojeski on the Video STEP 3 — STAGING THE CONCERT PERFORMANCE.

GIVE — Arm extended with palm down. Can also send the message "go," "go forth," "over there," "look," "afar," "there," "that place." It is a good gesture to indicate "This land that we are singing about," (in other words any land beneath this gesture).

Extended arm - palm down

TAKE — Extended arm with the palm up. Although very similar to the previous move it is amazing the different message that a simple turning over of the hand will send. This gesture can also be interpreted as "come," "I want," "give to me," "here, take this," "take my hand," "I need from you," etc.

Extended arm - palm up

These "give" and "take" moves can also be very effective using both hands for a different look.

Extended arms - palms up

Extended arms - palms down

See the musical example "Give Me Your Tired, Your Poor" from AMERICAN PORTRAIT, arranged by Ed Lojeski on the Video STEP 3 — STAGING THE CONCERT PERFORMANCE.

TRAVELING GESTURES — Here are a few moves that most viewers will immediately register as gestures that indicate movement or travel. You will notice that the same moves we use for these messages in real life often translate quite effectively to the stage.

- HITCH-HIKING — An actual dance of the 1950s and '60s the hitch-hike thumb can easily be incorporated into modern, country, or nostalgic songs that are talking about travel, moving, going to, etc. Consider phrases like "on the road again," "'way down in Louisiana close to New Orleans," "Go greased lightning," "Down to Highway 10 past a Lafayette," etc.

Hitch-hiking

- BASKETBALL "TRAVELING" ARMS — Sometimes the name of a move is taken from the gestures frequently used in everyday life, Consider, for instance, the "stop" and "go" signals that a traffic cop uses and that everyone recognizes. Similarly, signals that a referee or umpire utilize in their line of work are clear indicators of a specific message. We all know the signs for "touchdown!", "safe" and "you're out!" The arm movement that a basketball referee uses to signal a "traveling violation" is a churning of the arms like a knitter winding up her yarn. The move is very adaptable to both rock-and-roll music, and especially music of "the islands." Combine it with a "PONY" step and you will have a wonderful, and easy to execute, Caribbean routine. Experiment with this move to the refrains of such favorites as "UNDER THE SEA," "UNDER THE BOARDWALK" or "LIFE'S A TRIP!"

Traveling arms

THE SEARCH — When you are looking for something you shade your eyes from the sun with your blade hand to your forehead. In the 1960s and '70s this became a recognizable dance. It continues to send a similar message today and will come in handy if you find yourself trying to act out lyrics that reflect hunting, looking, watching or searching for anything.

The Search

WALKING OR RUNNING GESTURES — Put your feet together and alternatingly bend one leg after another. Performed slowly we call these "walking knee pops." With greater speed they are cleverly referred to as "running knees pops." As simple as it may seem, this is a very valuable move as many songs you will come across incorporate a message or at least a lyric about walking, running, leaving, strolling, coming or going.

Walking knee pops

Notice how the arms work in opposition throughout a walking knee pop just as they do when you are actually walking.

PARTNER KNEE POPS — In a traditional ballroom dance position, "walking knee pops" can present a very stylish dance that is appropriate for several periods of dance. Most often it is used with cakewalks, ragtime, Charleston and the various partnered dances of the turn-of-the-century.

Partnered knee pops

JAZZ RUN — A "Jazz run" usually implies that the dancer is moving across the stage in a slight plie. They are said to "running into the floor" as opposed to "on top of the floor." This is a very powerful looking run that can cover a lot of space in a short amount of time.

On top of the floor run

Jazz run into the floor

Notice how much further you get when you run staying close to the floor and extending the forward leg, long and low.

LEAVING THE AUDIENCE — This could be also described as cutting communication with the audience in order to change character. It refers to the many times in song and dance, and especially in choral medleys when your performers need to change character or mood between songs so that they can properly reflect the message of the new title. Sometimes, there will only be a beat or two between songs. Sometimes, nothing at all. One of the most effective ways to accomplish this change of character (without actually leaving the stage to change make up and costume) is by momentarily losing eye contact with your audience. This can be accomplished in many ways, a few of which are:

FOUR COUNT PIVOT — This series of eight steps can be performed at any speed but always consists of eight marching steps and four quarter turn pivots.

• Facing front, step forward on your left foot and pivot a quarter turn to your right as you step onto your right foot.
• Follow this with the left foot stepping directly toward stage right followed in turn by a quarter turn to your right so that you are now facing directly upstage.
• Now, step left directly upstage.
• Quarter turn to your right so that you are facing stage left.
• Step left toward stage left followed by a quarter turn to your right so that you are now facing directly down stage.

Notice that during those eight steps you could completely change character and be ready to perform the next routine.

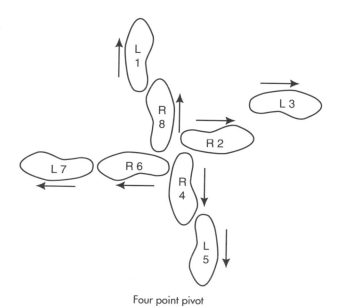
Four point pivot

TWO POINT PIVOT — This is another great transition move that involves only four steps but completely closes off eye contact communication with your audience in time for you to change your tune.

• Begin with a step (left foot) directly down stage toward your audience.
• This is followed with a full pivot to the right so that step "two" with your right foot has you facing directly upstage.
• Step three (left) goes upstage
• Follow with another pivot to the right that brings you all the way back to where you started.

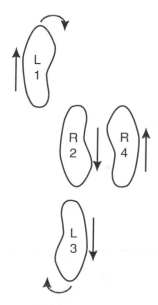
Two point pivot

Of course, either of these pivots could be performed turning to your left simply by stepping first onto your right foot and pivoting to your left.

PARTNERED PIVOTS — Try having a couple of dancers standing side by side execute simultaneous two point pivots beginning on their outside feet so that the first pivot is toward each other and the second pivot is away from each other. Eventually they will both return to face their audience.

PIVOTS IN A LINE — For another interesting visual effect, have a line-up of performers each do a full four point pivot each starting two beats after the dancer before them.

LUNGE PIVOT — This simply refers to a two or four point pivot that gives a lot more emphasis to beat one than any of the other beats. The performer literally lunges toward the audience on their first step and then, with less emphasis, finishes the pivot.

Partnered two point pivots - 1

Pivots in a line

Lunge pivot

Partnered two point pivots - 2

The best place to use pivots is where there is no singing going on because, obviously, as you lose visual contact with your audience you will also lose the clear vocal direction you have worked to maintain from the stage to your listeners. Still, how many times does a quarter note finish a sentence of the lyric with rests following on beats 2,3 and 4? By using beat one as the first step of your pivot you will not sacrifice any vocal communication on the silent beats of the measure.

PIVOT BURST — This is a pivot that incorporates a burst of the arms from high to low on beat one or on the first step. Sometimes a burst might be included on beat three in a two point pivot, or even on beats 1, 3, 5, and 7 of a four point pivot.

Pivot burst - beat 1

Pivot burst - beat 3

POUTING OR SHYNESS — Here are a couple of different moves that are sure-fire indicators for individual words or messages of shyness, pouting, etc.

• STEP TOUCH KNEES TOGETHER - With your hands behind your back and your knees absolutely together simply step to the left, turning your shoulders a quarter turn to the left as well. The "touch" of this step touch is really a light stomp or dig of the right foot after it has been lifted high and to the side on the first step. Repeat to the other side.

Pouting step touch

Female dancers in particular could also try this step touch with flexed hands to your sides hitting your raised heel as you step left or right. This will give you a cute dance reflective of the 1920s.

'20s Step touch

• FEET TOGETHER, ROCKING ON YOUR HEELS — With your hands behind your back and feet close together, rock the front of your feet from side to side in the same direction. This works great for songs like "Don't Sit Under The Apple Tree," "A Song Between Friends," or any song with that sort of walking beat. Try the same move holding hands with a partner for a sweet and innocent look.

Rocking on heels

PATRIOTIC MOVES — We are blessed with a plethora of fine patriotic songs in our country and so, can readily use a handy collection of moves and gestures to accompany them.

HAND TO HEART — This is an obvious signal of devotion and pride. Usually this move will have a cleaner look if your feet are exactly together.

Hand to heart

SALUTES — Although generally reserved for military-type songs such as "You're A Grand Old Flag and "Yankee Doodle Dandy," there are several variations of the traditional salute that can give it a more dramatic, comic, or dance-like flair.

• MILITARY SALUTE — palm down, fingers just above the right eye.

Military salute

• "GOMER PYLE" SALUTE — Made famous by Jim Nabors, this salute has the palm of the hand out toward the audience, making it a rather comical salute for modern audiences.

Gomer Pyle salute

• CHEST LEVEL SALUTE — A blade hand held at chest level gives the same proud feelings as a military salute without being so soldier-like.

Chest level salute

• 4-COUNT SALUTE — This involves making the very motion of the salute a dance step. This would never be tolerated in the actual ranks of the military, but, can be very energetic and effective when incorporated into a stage routine.

Beat 1 — Bring your right hand to your forehead in a traditional military salute.

4-Count salute - beat 1

Beat 2 — Bend your knees.

4-Count salute - beat 2

Beat 3 — Straighten your legs and extend your saluting hand overhead.

4-Count salute - beat 3

Beat 4 — Bring the salute hand to your side.

4-Count salute - beat 4

Try this salute, for instance, on the last measure of a song like "You're A Grand Old Flag" or on the "-ly" of "Born on the fourth of July" in "I'm A Yankee Doodle Dandy."

Another interesting way to use salutes is to do them in a peel or roll off-like a wave. A group of performers execute the salute beginning on successive beats. See the musical example "Battle Cry of Freedom" from AMERICAN PORTRAIT arranged by Ed Lojeski, on the accompanying video STEP 3 — STAGING THE CONCERT PERFORMANCE.

BELL ARMS — An individual, a couple holding hands, or a line of people holding hands, simply swing the hands forward and back like a bell. This can be done at varying heights and works very well for songs with a happy message as it looks like young children as they swing their hands while walking down the street. If performed very slowly it can also be quite a grand gesture.

- Try adding a step touch straight ahead to give the BELL ARMS more movement.
- Try a pattern that lifts the bell arms at gradually increasing levels with each lift. For instance, 1/4, 1/2, 3/4, full up. Between each lift, the hands would go back down to the starting position at your sides.

Bell arms

See the musical example "Toll the Bell of Freedom" from ALL AMERICAN, arranged by Mark Brymer on the accompanying video STEP 3 — STAGING THE CONCERT PERFORMANCE.

TRITE BUT TRUE GESTURES — Some of the most difficult words to choreograph are the ones that seem the most obvious at the outset but can come off quite "trite" if not performed in the proper fashion. For instance, every one recognizes that pointing to your self means "Me" and pointing at someone else means "you." Pointing toward the ceiling means "up," pointing at the floor means "down." Aren't you glad you bought a book to teach you all of that?

The challenge for a choreographer is to discover ways to make those universally recognized moves artistic while not sacrificing their intrinsic clarity.

YOU AND ME — Most of the time you will discover that ANY dance move can be effective if it is performed with total commitment and conviction. Pointing to yourself and then to your audience as you sing the words "me and you" will seem juvenile and silly unless it is performed with total heart.

- Notice how you can make more of a gesture by using both arms instead of one, or an entire hand as opposed to just the finger.

"Me and you" with both hands - 2

- Often it is the action of getting from one position to the other that will actually make a gesture "dance." For example, a sweeping arm from your chest out from one side to the other can include the entire audience in a "me and you" gesture.

Sweeping arm R to L

"Me and you" with both hands - 1

- Try pointing at the audience with your right hand as you step touch and face stage left .

"You" with step touch

- Do a lunge pivot that has you pointing at the audience on beat one. This is a very powerful way to say "you!" Do the same with your thumbs to your chest to dance "me!"

"You and me" with lunge pivot - 1

ALL — This is a gesture that can be done in several ways.

- A sweeping arm that "presents" the audience from left to right or vice versa can indicate "all" as in "all of you" or "everybody," or "the whole world!"

"You and me" with lunge pivot - 2

- Put both thumbs to your chest and one heel up to say a character-like "me!"

"Me" with heel up

Circular arm sweep - 2

"All" gesture

• A sweeping arm that makes a complete circle can dance beautifully and reflect both the musical line of a phrase and a message of inclusiveness.

Circular arm sweep - 3

Circular arm sweep - 1

85

Circular arm sweep - 4

Listening lunge

The message of your motions should be understood even if the audience were unable to hear the music to which you are dancing. Hence, a choreographer should usually begin with the most obvious gestures when he or she approaches the design of the dance.

A note placed on the third line of a G clef will always be a "B". It is up to the composer and the musician to make the note musical by varying it's length, volume, how it is approached, and how it is left. A dance move or gesture is exactly the same. Pointing to yourself will almost always mean "me." But a creative choreographer or dancer can make even this very simple move a beautiful and unique aspect of a performance.

HEARING or LISTENING — A hand to the ear will obviously give the message of hearing or listening. But can you make it dance more by lunging toward the sound that you are supposedly hearing? Notice how the opposite hand can be varied to extend the line of your dance pose or give your dancer greater strength with a fist.

SEEING or EYES — Again, the obvious gesture to indicate seeing or eyes is to point to your own eyes. But, there are a lot of ways to make that indication flow. Try, for example sweeping your jazz hands in front of your eyes as if revealing them for the first time.

See the musical excerpt "Zip-A-Dee-Doo-Dah" from A DISNEY SPECTACULAR, arranged by Mac Huff on the accompanying video STEP 3 — STAGING THE CONCERT PERFORMANCE.

A GOOD DANCE ROUTINE CAN TELL A STORY ALL BY ITSELF! — See how this is true in the following music examples on the accompanying video: "Supercalifragilisticexpialidocious" from A DISNEY SPECTACULAR Arranged by Mac Huff "This Land Is Your Land" from ALL AMERICAN Arranged by Mark Brymer (Included on the video STEP 3 — STAGING FOR THE CONCERT PERFORMANCE)

Listening

"Sweeping" eyes

Look at the way these few dance moves tell the story of the favorite Christmas carol "Up On The Housetop."

"Up on the housetop..."

"Out jumps good old Santa Claus!"

"All for the little ones Christmas joys!'

"Reindeer pause..."

"Down through the chimney with lots of toys!"

"Ho ho ho! Who wouldn't go!"

IT "FEELS" RIGHT!

When the lyric leaves room for interpretation, the trick is to discover the type of message you want to get across to your audience. For instance:

Disco music of the 1970s didn't necessarily tell much of a story or even attempt to give a specific message to the listener. In fact, dance music of many style periods was designed for the participants of the dance to simply feel good, (or at least hot and sweaty!). For a lot of choreographers, these are the most difficult dances to prepare for the stage since there is very little direction offered by examining the lyrics. Fortunately, however one only needs to visit a few dance clubs or view a few videos to build a reliable supply of dance moves of most any era that will adequately adapt to the stage. A waltz performed to the tune of "In The Good Old Summertime" or "Take Me Out To The Ballgame" does not further the story of the lyric but, it appropriately reflects the musical line and "feels" right to the performer and the audience.

This is not just true for light-hearted dances like disco, the Jitterbug or the Charleston. Consider the emotional base crucial for the success of traditional concert music, especially that of a spiritual nature. Moves of strength, inspiration, clapping, swaying are "feel good" moves that indeed enhance the performance of appropriate musical literature.

As an example, sing the song "America The Beautiful." When you get to the chorus, try these simple gestures that in some cases reflect the message of the lyric but in other cases simply "feel" right.

AMERICA! — Scoop your right hand from low to high.

"America" -1

AMERICA! — Scoop your left hand from low to high.

"America" - 2

GOD SHED HIS GRACE ON — Clap your hands together to "prayer hands" overhead.

"God shed His grace on"

THEE — Burst your hands from high to low reaching toward the audience.

"Thee"

AND CROWN THY GOOD.— Present open jazz hands low.

"And <u>crown</u> Thy good"

WITH BROTHERHOOD — Grab hands with your neighbors.

"With <u>brotherhood</u>"

FROM SEA TO SHINING SEA.— Lift those "held hands."

"From <u>sea</u> to shining sea"

Do you notice that the most important words are accented with appropriate moves? GOD is indicted by praying hands overhead. The two scooping gestures prior to that were just musically appropriate moves that got the dancer into position to accent the most important word with an appropriate gesture. (The underlined words from there on are the words in which the actual move should occur to give the most attention to key lyrics.)

See an example of this in "God Bless The U.S.A." arranged by Mark Brymer on the video STEP 3 — STAGING THE CONCERT PERFORMANCE.

Look how even the most simple movement can reflect a mood. An entire choir lightly tilting their heads from side to side shows contentment, cuteness, happiness, simplicity, for songs like "Simple Gifts," "We're The Choir" and "Grandfather's Clock." The moves do not have to be complicated or even numerous to be effective and appreciated.

See an example of this in "In The Good Old Summertime" and "Simple Gifts" from ALL AMERICAN on the video STEP 3 — STAGING THE CONCERT PERFORMANCE

PERIOD DANCES — A REFLECTION OF THEIR TIMES

Most of dance, at least the communicative part, is from the waist up. It might even be argued that the most important part of dance is from the neck up. There is no doubt that a singer/dancer's face is the most expressive part of their performance.

What makes choreographing dances of the "decades" easy is that the work has already been done for you. The dances were created by the public that participated in them at the time of their popularity. The good thing about recreating these dances in a choral setting is that all you are really trying to accomplish is a semblance of the actual dance of the time. You don't have to do a full-out Charleston in order for your singers to appear as though they are doing the Charleston in accompaniment to a song of the era. If you closely examine any of the period dance steps from "the waist" up and limit your choir's movement to those moves you will very often be able to create movement that resembles the original dance yet does not interfere with what you are trying to accomplish vocally. "Song-and-Dance" is neither just singing or just dancing. It is a wonderful collaboration of the two that winds up being an art form quite unique and legitimate unto itself!

Let's examine a few of the decades of Western dance and see what is going on that could be incorporated into your staged performances.

DANCES OF THE 1920s

WIDE PALMS — jazz hands with the palms facing the audience. This is reflective of the Charleston.

- Experiment with having them up at about shoulder height and simply swing them from left to right, like windshield wipers, as you would if you were doing a step-touching Charleston.

Wide palms - 1

- Try pushing them up into the air L-R-L-R or in patterns such as 4 times left, 4 right, 2 left, 2 right, 1 left, 1 right, 1 left, 1 right. The pushes should be on the beat.

Wide palms - 2

- Move the hands at chest level in opposition, working the elbow so that the hands go in, out, in, out.

Wide palms - 3

- Begin with the palms on your thighs and lift them up to shoulder levels like footless "Chugs."

Wide palms - chugs

Do you see how you could put together quite an interesting routine just by utilizing different combinations of these "wide palm" hand movements?

"BETTY BOOP EYES" — Wild frenzy or genuine excitement of the "roaring twenties" is best reflected in wide eyes with raised eyebrows. Again, this is where real communication happens and so must be rehearsed. Make these eyes a definite part of the choreography itself.

BRIGHT FACES — Can you think of other ways to make your faces bright and energetic? Try using the facial expressions that occur when you say the vowel sounds A, E, I, O, U. Which of them demonstrate excitement when applied to your face?

Here are the following obvious dance steps of the 1920s:

- THE CHARLESTON — alternating step touches with one touch forward followed by a step and touch behind. The hands are usually wide open, swinging side to side. However, a

Charleston could be accomplished with hands behind your back, holding your lapels, swinging overhead, in your pockets or many other creative variations. A CHARLESTON can be performed solo or with a dance partner in traditional "BALLROOM DANCE POSITION."

Charleston - 1

Charleston - 2

• STEP KICK — A variation of the Charleston could include making the front step-touch a step-kick and utilizing any or all of the hand options listed above.

• HOP KICK — A bit more athletic, the step becomes a "hop" and the kicks are on the off beat. Try the familiar 4, 4, 2, 2, 1, 1, 1, 1 pattern for a very high energy dance of the '20s.

Hop kick

• CHUGS — Hopping into the floor, usually with your feet parallel to each other and together. The "Chugging" motion comes from the little slide of your feet that happens when you jump "into" as opposed to "on top of" the floor. Generally, the hands are working in such a manner that before you jump they are placed palm-down on your thighs. Then as you hit the floor with the chug they come up to about shoulder level with the palms out. Like the feet, the hands are working parallel to each other. Other options would include having your hands clasped behind your back, holding onto the lapels of your coat, or putting your hands into your pockets. The chugs can easily be performed with a partner, facing them with held hands or even in traditional ball room dance position. Just make sure that when you are facing each other and are going to do simultaneous chugs you know which direction each of you is going so that you don't bump into each other's knees. If you both start to your left, this should solve the problem.

Try a pattern of chugs that is the familiar 4 left, 4 right, 2 left, 2 right, and 1 left, 1 right, 1 left, one right.

Chugs - single

Chugs - partnered

For a less athletic version of the "chug" step, try imitating the full-blown dance by bending your knees and duplicating the same hand moves as the above routine, but with no actual "hop" involved.

SHOOTING HANDS STRAIGHT INTO THE AIR — For a very energetic move that might or might not include feet movement, simply reach your hands up into the air either straight up or off to one side. Try the 4, 4, 2, 2, 1, 1, 1, 1 pattern.

This can be very effective when put in tandem with a BOX STEP or DOUBLE BOX STEP, a basic CHARLESTON STEP, or even simple marching.

Shooting hands straight into the air

GRAPEVINES — This is a pattern of walking steps on the floor that makes a weaving pattern moving the dancer across the floor.

- 8-COUNT GRAPEVINE — Always keeping your shoulders square to the audience, step first to the left and continue moving toward stage left as you step right across the front, left out to the side again, right behind the left, left out to the side, right across the front again, left to the side and end with bringing the right next to the left with a touch making it possible to reverse the routine and move back to the right.

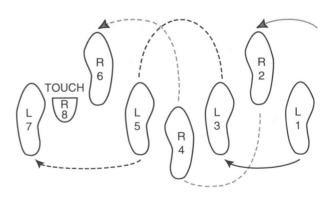

8-Count Grapevine

For a more rhythmic "grapevine" Try repeating the pattern with a dotted rhythm to your steps.

♪ ♩. ♪ ♩. ♪ ♩. ♪ ♩.
1   2   3   4   5   6   7   8

4-COUNT GRAPEVINE — In some ways easier to manage, the 4-count grapevine is the same as the 8 count except that it is half as long, covers half as much space, and requires half the amount of fancy foot work. Step first out to your left, cross front or back with the right foot, step left again and touch right on four. Again try this with both even quarter notes and a dotted rhythm.

♪   ♩.   ♪   ♩.
1   2   3   4

Try combining your 8- and 4-count grapevines for an extended routine. For instance, a 4-count to the left, a 4-count to the right, an 8-count to the left, followed by a 4-count to the right, left and an 8-count to the right will bring you right back where you began.

4 L - 4 R - 8 L - 4 R - 4 L - 8 R

GRAPEVINE ARMS — There are lots of possibilities for what to do with your hands and arms while your feet pull off a grapevine of any length.

For beginners you may want to simply put them behind your back or into your pockets. Or guys could hold the lapels of their jackets, the brim of their hat or the loops of their belts. Women could do any of the above or hold their skirt or parasol.

A little more experienced dancer may choose to hold their hands up in front of them, palms out toward the audience. Then, every time the feet cross the hands could cross and when the feet are apart the hands are apart.

Can you think of ways to make your grapevines country-western? 1940s? Caribbean?

'40s swing – 1

'40s swing – 2

Caribbean

SCISSORS or CUTAWAYS — Basically two names for the same or very similar steps. Cutaways describe hop kicks. On the hop the other leg bends bringing the foot behind the knee of the foot your are hopping on. The "kick" is out to the side, followed by a hop onto the "kicking" leg and a kick out to the other side by the original "hopping" leg. So there are really only two moves, a hop and a kick, repeated as many times as you want.

The hands are in a sense imitating the legs and feet. When the legs are crossed, so are the arms. When the foot is kicked the arms are extended. This "scissors' action by the arms can be done low and in front, or overhead.

Cutaways - 1

Cutaways - 2

DANCES OF THE 1940s

Most of our general vocabulary of dance steps can be used in the dances of the 1940s as they can in all of the decade dance styles. The important things to add are the stylistic characteristics that make it uniquely '40s.

As opposed to the frenetic action of the roaring '20s, the late '30s and '40s seem amazingly laid back and loose. The posture of the dancers was often more stooped and relaxed. Dances were performed low to the floor, with dangling arms and snapping fingers.

SWAY SNAPS — loose step touches with arms swinging to and fro, snapping fingers on each of the touches.

Sway snaps

BOX STEPS or JAZZ SQUARES — Performed mostly in plié with snapping fingers or flopping wrists and hands.

Box steps

4-COUNT GRAPEVINES — Again, low to the ground with somewhat stooped shoulders and snapping fingers, floppy hands or casual hands in the pockets.

'40s-style grapevines

Try many of your vocabulary of steps and try to make them feel 1940s. Use music like "Tuxedo Junction" or "In The Mood" to experiment with steps like the 2- and 4-point pivots, paddle wheel turns, and Lindy steps to create your own swinging routine.

Now try to modify those routines to make them compatible with a singing cast. Where can you leave off the foot work and make the motions of the upper body resemble the dances of the 1940s without actually infringing on what you are trying to accomplish vocally?

DANCES OF THE 1950s AND '60s

Draw from your collection of social dances of this era to create your unique choreographed routines.

THE SWIM — Standing in first, second, or "S" pose position do the backstroke, American crawl, the breast stroke, or even "Going down for the last time" for a recreation of the SWIM."

The Swim

THE MASHED POTATO — Knees together push, one foot down on the beat with arms flapping in unison. A good place for the 4, 4, 2, 2, 1, 1, 1, 1 pattern

The Mashed Potato

THE LINDY — Slide to the left followed by a back step, repeat to the right, shoulders always square to the direction you are facing. It works well with or with out a partner. Try it in ballroom dance position. Try it moving in opposition so that partners cross each other.

'50s-style Lindy

THE FREDDY — Like a "jumping jack," but more ridiculous! Two arms and one leg up on one, all down on two, other leg and both arms up on three, and all down on four.

The Freddy

THE PONY — Three steps almost in place (hop step step). Lots of variations of arms from lassos, to reins, bent wrists together overhead, flexed wrists at side.

The Pony

THE JERK — A dance move that consists of rib cage contractions on two and four following the arching of your back and pushing your chest out on beats one and three. The arms are usually alternating with one arm overhead and one low and behind on the first beat thrown forward on the contractions. Another option is to clasp hands together overhead and throw them forward on two and four.

THE MONKEY — Swinging your arms up and down like a monkey climbing up a tree. Any other actions that resemble an ape would be very appropriate.

The Monkey

HITCH-HIKE — If you are starting to see a pattern to the fact that the dancers of the 1950s and '60s developed dances from everyday movements the HITCH-HIKE ought to cement your notion. Stick out your thumb and pulse to the beat. Try moving the right thumb from stage left to right for four counts followed by the left thumb moving from right to left.

The Jerk

The Hitchhike

THE SEARCH — Hold a hand over your eyes as if you are looking for something in the distance. Again a motion that moves you focus from left to right and back again would be appropriate and musical.

The Search

THE TWIST — Get up on your toes and proceed to twist anything that moves. The feet can pivot back and forth, the hips and arms working in opposition. You can twist yourself all the way to the floor by bending your knees, or make it very "staged" by picking up one knee at a time and crossing it front of your body on specific counts, (try counts 1, 4 and 7, for instance.)

Like most of the other dances including the MASHED POTATO, THE PONY and THE LINDY, THE TWIST can be performed individually or with a partner.

The Twist

THE ALLIGATOR — There are two versions at least! Can you guess which one would be most conducive to singing?!

- Put one arm over the other in front of your face, open and close them like the jaws of an alligator.
- Lay down on your back with hands and feet in the air and wiggle them like an alligator on his back.

The Alligator

THE STAGING OF GOSPEL MUSIC

Everyone will have their own taste as to how much staging they find appropriate in gospel music performances. Some people may have very strong opinions as well. Like many of the other specialty selections the good news in gospel music is that tradition has built a reasonable amount of staging choices that are both appropriate and universally recognized. Here are few to consider:

SWAYS and CLAPS — Even a simple swaying from left to right can impact a musical and visual gospel selection. Practice sways that lead with the shoulder the direction that you are moving. You may want to practice this to the extreme and then back off for a subtle look once your dancers have captured the feel that the first thing to go left is the left shoulder.

In certain instances you will see gospel choirs turning their "straight-on sways" into subtle step touches. When this is the case, have your dancers back into the step touch so that when they step touch to the left they are actually facing down stage right and vice versa.

Gospel step touch

STAGE CLAPPING — Much of gospel music calls for slapping the sides of your legs or full-fledged clapping. It is important to remember that most of the time clapping is as much visual as it is aural. The "look" of the clap is at least equally important to the presentation as the sound it makes. Often you will want your claps to "look" louder than they actually are. This can be best accomplished by clapping the fingers only of one hand into the palm of the other. You can add to the visual impact by opening your hands and showing the hand to the audience when not clapped together.

Have fun experimenting with different frequencies of claps going on at the same time. For instance, have the men in your choir clap on beats two and four only. Gradually let the sopranos clap quarter notes on every beat of the measure. Eventually add the altos with eighth notes. The juxtaposition of all of these simple clap patterns is both energizing to listen to and interesting to watch.

Create more sophisticated clap patterns, to add more sophisticated percussion to your songs and dances.

EXPRESSIVENESS (and emphasis of musical line in sacred or gospel music) — The use of arm movements, changes in focus, walking patterns, etc., are great ways to make "physical" the music that you perform. This does not just apply to contemporary literature or music of a popular nature. Even historical, classical or sacred music can be enhanced by a more full use of the body in it's reproduction. The Dalcroze/Eurhythmic approach to creating music is all about expressing and learning about form, line, direction and musicality through "physicalizing" the notes on a page.

Experiment with a simple lift of an arm, a sweeping hand or series of visual focus changes to reflect and enhance the music you are rehearsing.

Most everyone has sung in a choir that sings the "Hallelujah" of Handel's HALLELUJAH CHORUS with great and inappropriate emphasis on the "JAH!" of the title word. As an experiment, have the chorus shoot a jazz hand into the air on the "HAL-" and drop it down as they finish the word. You will find that it is almost difficult to sing it the old way (with the accent on the last syllable) when you are so obviously accenting the first syllable with your movements. Once the new accents have become habit you will be able to leave off the arm movement if it offends, but the choir will sing the line more musically correct. In an instance such as this, movement has actually helped to present the music more effectively!

"Hallelujah"

Can you think of other songs where a sweep of the arm or some other small gesture can help your choir sing a musical line more effectively? Consider Kirby Shaw's JUBILATE DEO and SING HOSANNA. (See an excerpt of "Jubilate Deo" on the video STEP 3 — STAGING THE CONCERT PERFORMANCE.)

CRYING OUT TO BE STAGED!

Don't be limited by tradition when trying to keep your art form dynamic. The moments of risk will often times be when real electricity happens in your performances. Consider all of the other types of music (besides pop, Broadway, and historical dances) that are available to be staged.

- An opera chorus, such as "The Neighbor's Chorus" or "Stomp Your Foot Upon The Floor."
- A speech chorus or rap such as "The Geographical Fugue" or "Come To The Auction."
- Novelty numbers like "Hats," "Gloves," "Shades," "Cats," "Snack Attack," or "Rossini's Duet for Two Cats."

- Spirituals have always been great audience pleasers in a musical sense. Now you can work to make them more visually appealing as well. Consider what you might incorporate into a song like JERICHO by simply adding a series of head nods or head tilts. Experiment as well with peel-offs or ripples using a move as simple as a nod, a clap of the hands to "prayer position," or a change in visual focus. Sometimes a move that is nothing more than a hinge of the body from the waist, the knees or the ankles can be very musical and visually appropriate.

See the musical excerpt from "Jericho" arranged by Michael Dryver on the video STEP 3 — STAGING THE CONCERT PERFORMANCE.

Remember, just the suggestion of a motion can be effective. In other words, we go back to the notion that your choreography needs only to imply the move that the lyric or musical line indicates. A pull of the fist, a clasp of the hands, a clap-burst, a focus change can send a message to the audience of "power," "prayer," "sunshine," or "vision," respectively.

See "The Battle Cry Of Freedom" excerpt from AMERICAN PORTRAIT, arranged by Ed Lojeski on the video STEP 3 — STAGING THE CONCERT PERFORMANCE.

GESTURES

It is always important to consider "why" you are adding movement to the music you are presenting. Movement for movement's sake is rarely effective or even necessary, Instead it can actually detract from the artistic and emotional message that you are trying to convey.

It is usually a good idea not to force movement where it doesn't seem natural. At the same time it is a good idea not to resist or stifle physical expression when it feels natural. Two points to continually ask yourself as a staging director:

- Analyze the lyrics first. They are almost always the place to begin your physical interpretation of a song. Remember that you are trying to clarify the musical and lyrical message of your music, not muddy it up with unnecessary, random moves.

- Try to make the movement itself tell the story of the music. Remember the approach we took with "Up On The Housetop"? If the choreography is not literally translating the words into moves, is it at least reflecting the musical line? If not you may want to reconsider and start all over again keeping in mind the reason for your staging creation.

See the musical excerpt from "We Will Stand" arranged by Ed Lojeski, on the video STEP 3 — STAGING THE CONCERT PERFORMANCE. Notice how even very simple moves can work with both a large or very small ensemble.

An interesting and encouraging note for novice choreographers is the fact that it is often easier to manage effective choreography with a large cast than it is with a small one. If a small group of performers executes a simple move it will often have a very measured impact on the viewers. However, the same move performed by a large choir will have an amplified effect. Ten people swiftly raising their jazz hand above their heads will be fine. A hundred and ten choristers doing the same move will be profound in its visual impact.

DON'T BE AFRAID TO USE HUMOR!

Everybody loves to laugh, or at least smile! Staging a song can often help bring the natural, or even hidden humor out of a piece of music.

HIDDEN HUMOR — Try to look for the hidden humor that might add a new meaning to an old song. A twist of the lyrics, a play on words, an unexpected approach to a recognized standard are all possible in the magical world of live performance: "Frosty the Snowman" singing a Beach Boys surfing song, the smallest guy in the choir performing "Macho Man," the shortest guy dancing with the tallest girl.

See the musical excerpt "Kansas City" arranged by Mark Brymer on the video STEP 3 — STAGING THE CONCERT PERFORMANCE.

RECURRING HUMOR — It is often possible to incorporate a "running joke" throughout the performance. In one performance, for instance, we had Mr. Touchdown U.S.A. show up several times in the show only to be knocked down inadvertently by a cheerleader on each occasion. By the end of the show the audience was expecting the same joke when Mr. T finally caught on, ducked in time and got the girl! Not deep, but a lot of fun for all involved. See the musical excerpt of "Mr. Touchdown USA" on the video.

MAKING USE OF YOUR "BUFFOON" — Almost every cast is blessed with at least one natural comedian. Some are blessed with an entire stageful! It is important to turn this personality into

an attribute by highlighting this innate talent, or at least clever knack, into a positive part of your show. Make that person the Master of Ceremonies, the recurring "joke" or the hero of the day. See an example in the musical excerpt "A Whale of A Tale" arranged by Ruth Artman and "How Do You Do And Shake Hands" from A DISNEY SPECTACULAR on the video.

THE TEACHING PROCESS

Like teaching any subject effectively, it is important for staging directors and choreographers to have a logical process that will help their cast members learn their routines more quickly, retain them more accurately and perform them to the satisfaction of their teacher.

There are certain rules of order which generally work for most situations. Remember that when we were creating an approach to teaching dances steps we began quite logically with walking and moved on to more sophisticated concepts. Of course, you will want to remain flexible to accommodate unique casts and peculiarities of schedules and other variables. So, in what order does a stager of song and dance begin his or her instruction?

• First of all, there is a reason that we usually say "song and dance" as opposed to "dance and song." The singing should almost always be learned first. You cannot cover up bad or badly-performed music with all the flashy staging in the world. In fact, in most cases the music should be able to stand on its own before any movement is considered. However, once the music is learned to the point of being reasonably effective, one can move

onto adding movement to this already successful element. Be aware that the formula is very often:

Learn the music...teach the staging...relearn the music!

You shouldn't be discouraged by this very common equation. Your performers now have twice as much to remember compared to when they only had to worry about the singing. Also, don't spend eight weeks on the singing part of your performance and then expect the staging to fall perfectly into place in one evening's rehearsals. Both aspects of your show will take time and repetition to make their good quality become habit.

• Teach the repetitive parts of the song and dance first. As in the verse/chorus style of a song there will often times be repetitive parts of a dance routine. It is quite often a good idea to teach these chunks of staging first as you will be able to polish off sizable chunks of the song at the outset, plus there will be a reasonable degree of comfort for your performers every time that piece of material comes along.

• Teach fast. Even with beginning casts it is usually not a good idea to get bogged down in a few measures and spend frustrating amounts of time working to perfect them before you move onto the next section. Better to teach broad concepts and larger chunks right off the bat, even if some of your performers seem unable to keep up initially. This faster speed will allow those that pick up more quickly to actually rehearse their "performance" level when you later go back to bring the less experienced students up to their speed. They will also be able to assist in the teaching process by helping out the less experienced dancers. There is nothing more frustrating than a rehearsal that plods along. You can always go back and add more details once the general idea is "on" your performers.

• Make even your warm-ups seem like dance steps. Or, teach part of the dances as a warm up exercise that will eventually be used in one of your routines. For instance, a "jumping jack" is very much like "The Freddy," so it is a good warm up that can serve a dual purpose. Even certain stretching exercises for your legs, sides and arms can turn into effective dances. Using this vocabulary of steps that your performers already possess is a treasure house of movements for the staging director to utilize!

• Be certain to talk about the character or message of the movement that you are trying to communicate. Most of the time the dance steps are secondary to the personality of the song you are performing. From the very beginning of your rehearsals, try to have your performers work on characterizing their movement instead of simply marking through it. More often than not it is more important to make sure that the characterization of the staging is accurate, than it is to make certain a routine is technically perfect. Talk to your performers about the story you are trying to tell with the entire song, each verse and even every individual line of lyric. Notice how often your expression and attitude changes when you are holding a conversation with someone. Very seldom does your message call for a uniform expression on your face, one attitude or posture through out the dialogue. You change expression, posture and gesture with each new thought or idea, sometimes

as often as every word. In performance situations these changes of expression must be at least as varied, and MUST BE REHEARSED.

• Let your performers show their individual personalities even when performing unison choreography. Unless you are a military drill team or a precision pom pom squad, it is very seldom impressive for singers and dancers to perform with absolute uniformity. A stage full of audio-animatronic mannequins is not very creative, and is impressive to an audience for only a very short duration of time. It is possible to display individual personalities even while performing the same choreography. Most of the time this should be encouraged. An audience likes to feel as though they know the individuals on stage as characters or as human beings. By the end of the first song they should be aware of the unique character of each member of the ensemble in subtle or more pronounced ways. It is seldom a good idea to try to mask unique personalities. This potpourri of humanity is usually what will make a cast enticing to an audience.

This is not to say that choreography should not be drilled to the point of being "pinkie perfect" in its execution. However, once this is accomplished, allow individuality to give your routines true character.

• Use mirrors or a reflective surface when rehearsing movement. The use of these surfaces will cut your rehearsal time and increase your effectiveness by a great deal. First of all your performers will be able to watch themselves and your demonstration at the same time and from all angles. They will see both how the dance moves are performed

and the character that you have in mind for them. They will also be able to see their moves from an audience's point of view and be able to evaluate their own performance for strengths and weaknesses. They will see how their performance fits together with the rest of the cast and automatically adjust discrepancies, making the performance more accurate and clean. It is amazing to discover that some people will think that their arm is straight up in the air when it is really at an angle. A mirror will help them to analyze their position in space and adjust it with out the director having to point out every detail for every performer. Even if you cannot afford the expense of full length mirrors that will cover your entire cast, any reflective surface including windows or even some sort of tin foil will help significantly.

• As a director, it is not always a good idea to face your learning cast and attempt to mirror their movements so that they can follow along with you in reverse. For some students this will become very confusing and add to the inherent frustrations that can occur and stifle the learning process. It is usually better to turn your back on your cast and teach the dances initially facing the same direction that you want them to face. Then, they are truly mimicking your example. Give them a chance to learn it by your demonstration and description before you turn around to have a look. Then, as you watch them you may want to cue a move here and there to get them started in the right direction, as their translation of your moves is immediate and your reversal will not be a hindrance. An exception to this idea might be with very young performers who will not have the automatic tendency to try to second guess or translate what you really mean. With them a mirroring technique can often be very effective.

When you as the director or choreographer demonstrate a movement, be certain to do so exactly as you want it performed. Incorporate at least as much energy as you want your performers to incorporate. Use the facial expression that you deem appropriate each and every time. Every performer will not catch every detail of your demonstration from any individual run-through. You want to be sure that the time that they do catch it, they have caught what you had in mind. If you know the style, personality, energy level, and technique that you want, then demonstrate it that way!

• Incorporate videotaping to help your cast discover and analyze their strengths and weaknesses. Although this can be very time consuming and will often slow down your rehearsals more than the effort is worth, it can also be a very good way to show your performers on their own bodies what you have been talking about in regard to their performances. This can be especially effective for a show that has multiple performances. Like a football team reviews the films of their previous games to hopefully improve their next endeavor, so can a dancer analyze one effort to improve on the next.

TRICKS

Here are some effective "TRICKS" that seem to always work and can be used in more traditional concert settings as well as full- blown song and dance performances.

PEEL-OFFS — Other names include "waves," "ripples," "domino effect,"

etc. Basically all it means is that one person or group of people do an action that is followed immediately by the next group or individual doing the same motion and so on down the line until every one has completed the act like the falling over of a line of dominoes. PEEL-OFFS can start from one end of the stage and move to the other, from both ends and meet in the center, from front to back, middle to the side or even from down to up if you like.

These "PEEL OFFS" could be performed:
• Individually, one person at a time.
• In pairs, or small groups. For example, in a song with four bar phrases you might have each of four groups do the move, one group per measure. Or, you might decide to have them perform the move a move on each count of a single measure.

Some very simple gestures that work effectively as "PEEL OFFS" include:
• Nods
• A simple step from first position to second
• Salutes
• A change of focus or change of body angle
• A use of a longer dance routine that simply begins a beat or two or more later than the initiating group.
• Marching steps
• 2- and 4-POINT PIVOTS make simple and effective "peel off" routines

See the musical examples "We've Got A Show For You" by Lisa Lauren Pollack and "Boogie Woogie Bugle Boy" arranged by Mark Brymer on the video.

THINK DIMENSIONAL! — Making use of all of your options related to height, depth and width can greatly enhance the visual end of your choreographed

performances. It is indeed a pain to haul around risers and platforms for performances that are on the road. But, by adding the dimension of height to your efforts you have really made it worth the effort. Remember, you're the director and you have plenty of helpers in the cast. You simply have to direct the operation, not "schlep" the heavy gear!

Sometimes, the simple use of a couple of ladders, stools, boxes or even hay bales is sufficient to make your performances sink or soar. Also, don't forget the "human elevators" we were all blessed with at birth...our knees!

RESTS — Fill in the rests to emphasize a rhythm.

• The easiest, and often most suitable place to add choreography to a song is during a dance break, even if that dance's "break" is only one beat long. "Rests" are a good place to look when you first start analyzing a piece, looking for ways to stage it most effectively and ensuring that the movement does not get in the way of the music. When some choreographers see music they look immediately at rests, especially quarter and eighth note rests, as opportunities to clap, snap or whack.

• When that same choreographer sees two or three beats of rests they realize that there is an opportunity to make several clapping sounds or lose temporary visual contact with the audience through the use of a pivot or turn. When there are no words or notes to sing there is greater opportunity to dance with less regard to keeping the voice pointing toward the audience. The ends of phrases or during transitions between songs are great places to look for turns, clap patterns or full dance-break routines.

BEST PERFORMERS — Put your best performers in the most visible place on stage. This seems rather obvious if you are indeed aware where the most visible place to your audience IS on stage. Many times it will be downstage center. If your strongest performer is placed there the eyes of the audience are automatically drawn to that person. It is amazing how what the audience sees front-and-center is what they surmise is happening with the rest of the cast, even if in truth, the rest of the cast is performing somewhat less exacting routines.

You should, however, be aware that downstage center is not always the most visible place to the biggest portion of your audience. During rehearsal be sure to move around your performance viewing area so that you have a clear picture of what your full audience is watching. Your vantage point at the front of your choir may not be the same view that a person far stage left or in the mezzanine has.

LESS IS MORE — Sometimes "less is more." There is a lot of truth to this old showbiz adage. Especially when it comes to choreography and staging, it is often the case that fewer moves make stronger statements. This is particularly true when it comes to staging the male dancer but is also true for designing dance routines in general. Don't be afraid to edit your own creations to make sure that they achieve what you want with the least amount of distraction.

MEAT GRINDERS — This is a rather graphic name for a pattern of movement on-stage that has intersecting lines moving back and forth in opposition either downstage and up, or left and right. It is a very good example of how a very simple walking pattern of four steps forward and four back, performed in opposite patterns, can be very interesting to watch and simple to perform.

See "God's Country" arranged by Mark Brymer on the accompanying video.

AUDIENCE PARTICIPATION — It is often very effective for a cast of performers to break the fourth wall between themselves and their audience, encouraging the audience to actually participate in, rather than merely observe, the performance. It is usually a good idea to let your audience know that you know that they are there. You can do this by having them get involved at one or many points in the show.

• SHAKE HANDS — Sometimes as simple a move as going into the audience to shake a few hands and say "hello" will suffice in getting that audience to feel as though they know you and that they now have vested interest in having the show be a success. After all, now it is not merely a stage full of performers that they are watching, but rather a stage full of new friends.

• CLAPPING ALONG — Although it can be annoying to an audience who is constantly being told to "put your hands together," most people like to clap or stamp on occasion if it doesn't last too long and the music is appropriate. Don't necessarily count on your audience to keep a steady beat, not rush and clap on the offbeats. Your cast must be disciplined enough not to rush with them if they do, or go with the natural tendencies of the crowd.

• SING-A-LONGS — Most people enjoy a good sing-a-long especially if they really know the song. Sometimes the use of audience cue cards or follow the bouncing ball techniques will help in both the audience's comfort zone and the visual interest of that portion of your show.

• A GUINEA PIG — It is a lot of fun for everyone to have someone in the audience singled out and made to be a part of the show. Dress up the principal or the mayor like Santa, Rudolph or Uncle Sam. Pick a man or boy to sit on a stool in the middle of the stage while all the girls sing to him, or put a woman there and let the guys sing to her.

• DANCE-A-LONGS — It is a lot of fun to get the audience involved in the dancing, too! This works especially well for waltzes, the Twist or even the Limbo. The performers have to be the aggressive ones to get people out of their seats, and safely back when the dance is over.

HIGHLIGHT THE UNIQUE PERSONALITIES OF YOUR GROUP — There is almost always a buffoon in every cast, or maybe a better term is "class clown" or "comedian/ comedienne." Instead of a seeing this person as a detriment to your efforts, look at them as another opportunity to add character to your show. There is almost always a place where you can highlight that special quality by way of a solo, a speech, a dance or even just a very short comic "bit" to let this individual shine!

But this method of showing off the unique members of your cast need not be exclusively reserved for comic relief or buffoonery. Try to find out what other "gifts" lie hidden in your ensemble. Very often there will be an impersonator who can introduce every song in your performance using a different character from his or her repertoire. There may very well be a juggler, an acrobat, a poet, a baton twirler, or somebody who plays a common or even uncommon instrument that could be incorporated. Wouldn't it be great to have your singer/dancers suddenly begin playing horns or drums, harmonicas or fiddles, even combs and kazoos?! It is a very good idea to ask your cast when you are first developing your show for any skills or gifts they have to offer and then begin to consider whether there is a proper place to implement them in your show.

See the musical excerpt from "God Bless The U.S.A." arranged by Mark Brymer on the video.

MANY ARMS ON ONE BODY —
This refers to the appearance given to the audience when two or more dancers line up directly behind one or the other. When they move their arms in opposition it looks as though the front person has many arms connected to their one body.

• Try this with simple jazz hands at varying levels.

Many arms - jazz hands

• Another fun look is to have bursts from high to low and low to high happening simultaneously.

• "L" ARMS at varying angles with blade hands.

Many hands - "L" arms

• Alternating floppy wrists at varying levels will give an active swing feel and look for a song like "It Don't Mean A Thing" or "Shakin' The Blues Away."

Many arms - floppy wrists

• EAST INDIAN/ORIENTAL ARMS —
Either praying like a standing Buddha or with bent wrists like an exotic Thai dancer, this particular "many arms one body" can be fun and a genuine curiosity.

Many arms - Oriental

CHOOSING MUSICAL ARRANGEMENTS

Maybe you are lucky enough to have an arranger who designs their work to perfectly suit your cast. More often than not, however, people rely on professional arrangers who are writing for the "unknown " choir or performing cast and and whose arrangements are published through national or international publishing houses. They will not have had the benefit of knowing what unique qualities your group possesses or even what hurdles you may have to overcome in your particular situation. It is your prerogative and your responsibility as the director to make sure that the arrangements that you eventually perform with your group are singularly appropriate for them. Sometimes that will mean that you can purchase an arrangement from a professional or their publishing company and use it exactly as it is. On other occasions you may get that arrangement and then tailor it to your needs. Just because the published arrangement has five verses and six choruses does not mean that you have to perform all five and six! If you want to do one of each or mix them around that is totally up to your taste and preference. Just remember that if you want to make substantial changes to the songs, you must first obtain permission from the copyright owner.

• REVUES — It is not a difficult task to put together an act or an evening of entertainment that has a broad or even a very narrow theme to it. It does not take a showbiz wizard to weave together songs with topics of any relation. Think of the seasons, months, holidays, sports, vacations, places, modes of transportation, periods of time like a specific year, a decade or an era. The list is absolutely unlimited. Brainstorming the numbers to include in such a revue, jostling them around to get the effect you desire and fine-tuning them in rehearsal can be some of the most rewarding moments of any show production.

• BEING ECLECTIC — If you are working in educational circles, you should put an emphasis on being eclectic. Even if you are not working with students, it ought to be a priority to expose both your performers and your audiences to a broad spectrum of musical experiences. Few people like to know in advance exactly how a movie or book is going to end when they sit down to watch or read it. The element of surprise is often what can keep them attentive and enjoying their experience. There is rarely a need, or even a call for, an entire concert of one style of music or one style of dance. Two hours of Broadway show stoppers will soon leave an audience bored and even hostile. So will two hours of almost anything that is simply too similar. Luckily there is no need for such uninspired programming. There are so many quality choices of music and dance in any of the abundant styles of music . They are all compatible. There is absolutely nothing wrong with mixing twentieth century music with music of the Baroque period. There is no reason you cannot go from rock and roll to stand and sing, from madrigals to speech chorus, from opera choruses to French motets. Music is such a dynamic and varied field that if anybody goes away bored or apathetic there is definitely something wrong with our programming.

FINAL THOUGHTS

• DARE TO BE DIFFERENT — You don't always have to have your tallest boy dance with your tallest girl. You don't always have to begin your performance with an up tempo number and end your show with a kickline. Use your unique talents and the talents of your unique cast to make every show you design, rehearse and perform exceptionally yours! See "I've Got No Strings" from A DISNEY SPECTACULAR arranged by Mac Huff on the video.

DIALOGUE — Include dialogue to show another dimension of your performers and to personalize your performance. Most audiences want to feel as though they know the performers on stage personally. This is especially true in a show where the performers are basically playing themselves and not some imagined characters. One of the most effective ways to accomplish this relationship with your audience is to hold a conversation with them. When a cast member steps forward and speaks directly to the audience to introduce the next song, thank them for their attendance or for any other reason, they are opening the door for a more personal relationship with their audience. This is not to suggest that there must always be an "Ed Sullivan-style" approach to every show. But, talking occasionally, reading a poem, telling a joke or a story, performing a skit or talking about the music you are offering to your guests is often greatly appreciated.

MOVEMENT CAN ENHANCE WHAT WE'VE BEEN DOING WELL ALL ALONG — "If it ain't got heart, it ain't art!" Adding movement to what you have been doing successfully with choral music need not be seen either as a compromise or a cop out. There will always be times when the most effective way to perform a work of choral art is to simply stand still and sing. Movement is fortunately another choice that is available to us.

Costumes, lighting, publicity, special effects and, yes, even choreography are valid options when it comes to the high quality performance of choral music. "Heart," however, is not!

Some would argue, in fact, that the only essential ingredient in art, that which separates it from mere noise, is the emotion that it emits. A conscientious artist or stage director would also agree that the emotional core that is the heart of the art must be rehearsed as much as the diction, the tone quality, the phrasing and the cut offs. But how does a staging director manage to get the cast members to rehearse the kind of emotion that he or she has in mind for each nuance of the performance? This is a very real problem and one that is not easy to answer in black and white terms, after all, we are talking about some fairly ethereal territory when we begin to talk about individual and group emotion. Trying to predict the reaction of our varied audiences is another immense challenge. Still it is an important part of the director's many responsibilities. At least you should have in mind what you hope your audience will feel and how you think your performers will be able to serve as catalysts for those emotional responses.

Performers should understand that it is never satisfactory to wait until the actual performance itself to practice each and every aspect of your performance, especially the emotional elements! Your audience is your "guest." You have "invited them" to witness your work of art and you can expect their undivided attention. They can expect that you will value their time and attention to the extent that you will not waste an instant of it by offering them anything less than your utmost. If you have not fully rehearsed any single element of your performance you are cheating your audience. This includes abundant rehearsal of facial expression, transitions, bows and, most of all, emotion!

How do you rehearse emotion?

We have already talked about the different messages specific postures or gestures send to the audience. A wide second position sends a strong statement, an upturned hand can mean "come," "please give," or "help." Every performer must experiment with what they do physically when they genuinely feel any given emotion. When you feel joy or confidence how are you holding your shoulders and rib cage? When you feel despair what do you do with your hands or even your eyes? These are valid questions to ask yourself when analyzing your performance. You should try out many options and figure out which will be the most effective or which will best get your message into your art, just like you do with musical and choreographic nuance all the time. This should be some of your most exciting rehearsal time, for where heart is being used and experimented with, vivid art is apt to occur!

TAKE RISKS — Make sure that you are always willing to take some risks. Go out and experience your art as well as observing it. Participate in all the new directions that are so important to any dynamic art form. Taste new tastes, touch new realms, explore new avenues that will help you to better express and illuminate our human condition. This is what art can do. This is what song, this is what dance and YES! This is what "song and dance" can do!

MOVEMENT AND STAGING FOR THE YOUNG CHOIR

Singing and dancing certainly need not be reserved for secondary students and adults. The younger children want to be involved, too. Everybody knows how difficult it can be to get a third or fourth grader to stand or sit still. So, you might as well take a crack at controlling that wiggling and calling it choreography! With these younger students you may not want to do as much full scale dance. Perhaps more positioning and a degree of "choralography" will suit your young cast better. Here are some basic physical moves and stage designs (some repeats, some new) that have been found to work especially well with younger students.

BASIC FORMATIONS

RISER FORMATIONS — Here are some simple alternatives to the basic block formation we that work well on choral risers.

• Bowling pin formation — One person in the front row, two in the second, three in the third, etc., as big as you want it to be. The row behind is always standing in the windows (between the shoulders) behind the row in front of them. Experiment with having the "point" of the this formation upstage and the wide part downstage for a change. Also, this could be set up at an angle, or with different focus options for many different looks.

Bowling pin formation

• STAGGERED (in the windows) — This is basically a "block formation" but with space between each person in each line. It can be built by having everyone stand in any number of rows and then having every other person take a step forward or back so that you are left with twice as many rows and space between people.

Staggered formation

DIAGONAL LINES — Performers should line up off the shoulder of the next performer and upstage or down. This will form diagonal lines. Again, changes in the visual focus of the group will change the look of these diagonals.

Diagonal lines

• HALF CIRCLES — Whether one or many, convex or concave, half circles can be a nice visual change from a square or triangular formation. Notice how easy two half circles can become one big circle for another staging possibility that gives a look of universality and brotherhood.

Half circles - 1

Half circles - 2

• STAGGERED HALF CIRCLES — Similar to the way a solid block formation can loosen up by having every other person take a step forward or back to double the number of rows, the same can happen to one or more half circles to give a new and spacious look to your choir. Notice how much bigger your choir looks now that there are twice as many rows and the performers have room to move.

• FAMILY PORTRAIT — This refers to any formation that resembles a pose that a family assumes when attempting to have a group photo taken. Some are sitting, some kneeling, some standing, etc. Notice how body contact between performers makes the entire formation look a lot more friendly to the audience.

Family portrait

FUN AND CREATIVE FORMATIONS

There are unlimited possibilities when it comes to building a formation of humans onstage in something other than a geometric shape like a square, circle or triangle. Sometimes the lyric or subject matter of the song will spark an idea of a new formation. For instance, for a song about a show boat, it is possible to place cast members in such a way that three or four look like the paddle wheel, two more make the smoke stack and the rest of the cast fills out the bulk of the boat itself. Here are a few of the many possibilities.

SHIP/BOAT

• A VIKING SHIP — Have the choir line up in two rows perpendicular to the audience. The front and back of the rows should stay side-by-side while the rest of the line gradually bows out and back together again. The front of the ship could even have one person leaning forward like the mast head of an ancient ship.

Viking ship

• ROW BOATS/LONG BOATS — Have several people sit on the floor with their feet and legs apart, bent at the knees as though they were sitting in a toboggan. They can reach and row together like the crew of a long boat. This same formation could work for a sled ride in a wintry number. See if you can pull yourselves along with your heels as you row so there is actual movement to your row boat look.

Row boat

• SHIP — In a parallel line to the audience, a row of performers can begin and end with one standing. The next person is slightly stooped and the next a little more until you get to the middle of the line where the performers are actually kneeling on one knee. Everyone can face the same direction and row with imaginary oars for a look that resembles a canoe. You can even have passengers in this boat by having them stand upstage of the boat in the lowest section of the line. This boat can also move along the floor with a step and a drag of the knee.

Ship

• A BOAT ON THE RISERS — Sometimes you can get the feel and look of a boat simply by having the entire cast face one direction and put their upstage foot up one step of the risers. Then they can row and get the semblance of a boat full of paddlers.

For examples, see the musical excerpts of "Happy Music In The Air" by Ruth Artman and "A Whale Of A Tale" arranged by Ruth Artman on the accompanying video STEP 4 — MOVEMENT AND STAGING FOR THE YOUNG CHOIR.

OTHER TRANSPORTATION FORMATIONS

• BUS — Two rows of two side-by-side and perpendicular to the audience resembles a bus with the prerequisite aisle down the middle. Put one person up front on a stool to look like the driver.

Bus

• CARS — The performers stand two by two. You can have one or several cars moving around the stage at the same time.

Cars

• TRAINS — Long lines of performers, some could be facing each other like they are sitting in a dining car.

Train

• SUBWAY — Everyone face one direction and hold up your upstage hand as though you are grabbing a balancing strap.

Subway

For examples of this technique, see the musical example "California Here I Come" from the revue ALL AMERICAN arranged by Mark Brymer.

• RIDING A HORSE — Spread your feet apart wider than your shoulders, bend your knees a little bit and hold your hands close together in front of you as though you are holding onto the reins of your horse. Now plié on every other beat for a slow song or every beat for "Yankee Doodle."

If some ride the horse as shown above and another behind them holds onto their waist, it can look like the rider has a friend along riding behind them.

• A CARRIAGE RIDE — Two people side by side, either sitting or standing each with their knees together. One of them could pretend to hold the reins of the horses while the other holds the drivers arm. You could even put some more performers out in front of them to pretend to be the horses themselves. This can also give the look of a sleigh ride and is great for songs like "Jingle Bells" and "Over The River And Through The Woods."

Riding a horse - 3

Riding a horse - 1

Carriage ride

Riding a horse - 4

Riding a horse - 2

111

• THE CATERPILLAR — A whole line of performers standing close together and facing the same direction. They can hold onto each others waist, shoulders or elbows to connect like a many segmented caterpillar. This can be a lot of fun with a skating step, or even doing "the wave" while all connected.

Skaters - 2

The Caterpillar

• ICE SKATING — Putting your hands behind your back and pretending to skate as individuals can be very effective. You can also hold hands with a partner in the traditional skater's grip, or in long lines holding onto the waist of the person in front of you. This can be the entire staging and choreography for a song like "Winter Wonderland" or "Let It Snow!"

Skaters - 3

For a musical example, see "We Need A Little Christmas" from the revue I LOVE CHRISTMAS arranged by Ed Lojeski on the video STEP 4 — MOVEMENT AND STAGING FOR THE YOUNG CHOIR.

Skaters - 1

112

• A SLEIGH RIDE — Have the entire choir sit and/or kneel very close together on and in front of the risers. They should line up directly behind one another as if they are crowded into an open-air sleigh. You could have a team of reindeer or horses out in front pretending to pull the load. Sometimes a formation like this will be more recognizable if it is set up at an angle rather than directly facing the audience.

Sleigh ride

• HUMAN OCEAN — This can be represented with many rows of singers at increasingly higher levels. The front could be kneeling with their rears on their heels, the next row kneeling but off their heels, the next row squatting, etc., to accomplish this gradual heightening. Have each row sway the opposite of the row in front of them for a watery, undulating surf. You could even have a suspended swimmer float by, or "Jaws" himself for a little added humor to your ocean picture.

• "MANY SITTERS/ONE CHAIR" — One person kneels, the next in line sits on that knee, the next sits on the lap of the last person sitting, and so on for as long as you want the line to last. This is not difficult even though it may appear so. The trick is to make sure that everyone is holding only the weight of one other person. It is important to get a straight and solid leg in position for the next sitter to light on. This can be a very funny picture to the audience especially on a song like "Together Wherever We Go" or "We Go Together."

Many sitters/one chair

For a musical example see "Together Wherever We Go" arranged by Ruth Artman on the video.

PROPS

Props are an easy and fun addition to the visual end of your production. With young performers they can give a semblance of "showbiz" while not always demanding great skill and agility to handle effectively.

Some of the most accessible and relatively inexpensive props that work on stage are:

• STREAMERS — Streamers can be made of either ribbon, strips of crepe paper or some other material. Sometimes these streamers can be attached to short sticks or doweling rods for easier handling.

• SCARVES — Scarves are usable both as a costume accessory and as a prop. Some scarves are so light weight that they can actually be juggled, but more often than not dancing and swinging them in simple patterns is their best use.

• HULA HOOPS — Everybody loves to try their waist at hula hoops. They can add a lot of color and movement to songs of the fifties and sixties and also make great frames for a couple of singers to peer through on a poodle-skirt ballad.

• SKATE-BOARDS AND ROLLER-SKATES — These are great for simulating ice skating or surfing or for novelty numbers in their own right.

• FLASHLIGHTS — There couldn't be an easier prop that gives you better bang for your buck than a simple flashlight. Cover them with green and red cellophane and they'll appear to the audience like lights on a Christmas tree. Hold them under your chin for an eerie macabre look. Hold them upright to look like a candle. Try "peel offs," waves and flickers for memorable and illuminating moments on stage.

For a musical example, see "It's Christmas Time" by Ursulene McCamley included on the video.

• HATS — Top hats, derbies, head bands, skimmers (ice cream hats), stocking caps, baseball caps, pith helmets, hats are an easy way to create a period piece or more.

• SHOES — You may not initially think of shoes as a prop as much as a costume element, but if something you need can serve a dual purpose why not make the most of it. Tap shoes and ballet slippers are obvious. But, try

having some of your cast members put their shoes on their hands, hide behind the choral risers and do a routine to the tune of "42nd Street" or "Give Me That Ol' Soft Shoe" with their hands doing the "stepping."

• SUNGLASSES — Nothing changes a young performer's behavior and even personality more quickly than by having them don a pair of "shades." It's amazing how uninhibited they become and how open to more relaxed performing. Plus, sunglasses can look like a lot of fun and help characterizations come alive.

• GLOVES — If you want to draw attention to hand movements gloves can really set off and make exciting even the simplest of hand choreography. Experiment with different colored gloves. Try white or florescent gloves under a black light for a very dramatic effect. Paint the front half of your gloves a different color from the back and see all of the new possibilities for splashes of color on stage. Gloves can be sequined, fingerless, elbow length or short, any of a countless list of possibilities.

For a musical example, see "Gloves" by Hank Beebe on the video.

CALCULATED EMOTIONAL APPEAL – It can sometimes be a formidable challenge for a director to convince any performer to practice and display certain emotions on stage. This is especially true for revealing human emotions such as love, brotherhood, inspiration, etc. And this is especially true when it comes to working with young performers. Asking a fourth grade boy to hold the hand of a fourth grade girl and pretend to enjoy it is just short of asking him enjoy wearing a coat and tie at the 4th of July picnic! The

key, however, to demonstrating emotion on stage is that all that matters is the impression that comes across to the audience. What the performer is actually feeling is basically irrelevant. You as a director must be able to teach your performers to look the part, to portray the emotion whether they are comfortable with it or not. This takes careful calculation and an eye for what the physical elements are that convey a particular emotional message.

• HOLDING HANDS — If you want your performers to hold hands and appear to the audience as though they are enjoying the experience, then consider what the moves are that one would normally carry out if one actually WERE enjoying it. For instance, have your performers walk up to each other, look at each other's nose, look at each other's hand, grab that hand, look back the other's nose and then look at the audience. To the young performer the choreography for this number is to walk, look at nose, look at hand, grab hand, look at nose, look at audience. To the audience the picture is of a young couple affectionately and sincerely holding hands and liking it. Many emotions can be approached in this manner quite effectively.

Please see the musical example "Just One Person" arranged by Mark Brymer on the video.

• SIGN LANGUAGE — Any alternative language can be a beautiful and fascinating element to a musical endeavor. Sign language is the only one that is also beautiful visually. Generally, slower songs are good ones to begin to use sign language for the choreography, but it need not be left exclusively for that. Believe it or not, some deaf people talk amazingly fast! There is usually a sign language expert in your school or community that would love to help you and your cast develop a sign language vocabulary and repertoire. There are excellent and easy to use dictionaries in almost any library. It is still a good idea to check your choices with an experienced signer but you really can get a good start on your own with one of these resource books. Remember as you design your sign language choreography that you are trying to get the meaning of the words across to your "listeners" and that you must be careful not to be insensitively literal in your translation of the lyrics. This is another reason to enlist the aide of an expert. They can help assure that you are saying what you and the lyricist had in mind.

Sometimes it is effective to only have one person on stage at a time doing the sign language, but an entire choir of signers is an impressive sight to behold! Some of the best songs for beginner signers are "Somewhere" from WEST SIDE STORY, "He Ain't Heavy, He's My Brother," "You Are So Beautiful," "Everything Is Beautiful," "Heal The World," "We Are The World," "Silent Night" and many others.

• RE-ENACTING REAL LIFE MOMENTS ON STAGE — Spend some time reflecting on the events that happen in real life that leave an indelible emotional imprint on your heart and mind. Many people will come up with very similar reminiscences. Why not try to recreate these universal moments on-stage arousing in your audience those remembered feelings. Who is not touched by a small child holding a balloon or greeting a puppy, opening a gift or walking hand-in-hand with a new friend? These can be easily staged for calculated and predictable emotional moments from the stage.

• SLIDES — A slide show that uses related photos to accompany your music can be another visual trick to enhance just the right program selection. For a graduation show for instance you might include baby pictures of those who are graduating. For a patriotic show you might include photos of famous natural sites or famous patriots.

• FOCUS — Focus refers to the calculated use of visual focus, and in this case simply means that where your performers are looking can be one of the most powerful tools you as a stage director have at your disposal. Notice how inspiring it appears when your cast all looks

at one spot, say at the back of the auditorium above the audience's heads. It might be as simple as the exit sign above a door or the the light booth. All eyes focused on one location is mesmerizing to the audience and gives a look of vision and determination.

Focus over the heads of the audience ("exit sign")

Try some other experiments with focus. Have the entire cast look slowly from stage left to right as they sing a phrase like "O beautiful for spacious skies, for amber waves of grain...."

Have the cast look from low to high as they sing "It's curtain time and away we go, another openin' of another show!"

Have the cast look from right to left with an arching motion as if you were following the path of a rainbow.

Notice how easy it is to throw the audiences attention to a soloist or to a certain area of the stage if everyone on that stage is looking at that spot.

Focus - downstage left

Look how each performer becomes an individual if they all chose their own focus point. This can give a very effective feeling of pensiveness or introspection even within a crowd of performers.

See the musical example "It's Christmas Time" by Urselene McCamley on the video.

SPOTLIGHT SPECIAL TALENTS

With any age group, but especially with younger performers it is a good idea to highlight the special talents or training of your young performers. Even with very amateur casts, and maybe especially with them, parents want to see displayed what they have been supporting through Saturday morning dance classes and piano lessons. Your job as a director is to become aware of these attributes and put them to use.

Here is a short list of specialties that almost every cast has one or more of, sometimes quite unwittingly:
- Ballerina
- Tap dancer
- Some other specialized dance like clogging, jazz, etc.
- Pianists
- Other instrumentalists
- Jugglers
- Acrobats
- Baton Twirlers
- Break Dancers
- Ventriloquists
- Mimes
- Comics
- Impressionists
- Magicians (For a musical example, see "Old Sue's Panda" by John Carter and Mary Kay Beall on the video.)
- Speaker, actor or actress, master of ceremony — these are legitimate talents at your disposal!

For a musical example, see "Dixieland Jamboree" arranged by Kirby Shaw on the video.

DANCE WITHOUT MOVING THE FEET

Young performers very often have considerable difficulty managing intricate dance steps, especially if they involve a lot of fancy footwork. In truth, these are very seldom the most effective performance choices for them anyway. Remember that song and dance is unique in that the movements need only resemble the actual dances of an exclusively dance ensemble. There are many dance "steps" or moves that you can use with your young performers that look like the real dance but are much easier and will not do damage to your vocal product.

• HITCH-HIKING — This is the 1950s and '60s move that is simply "thumbing it" from left to right to the beat of the music. This can be done with feet together, apart or in an easy "S Curve" position.

Hitch-hiking

• THE SWIM — Feet planted in second or first position, move the arms like the breast stroke, the American crawl, the backstroke, or any other swimming move you can imagine.

The Swim

• DROWNING — Plug your nose, raise a few fingers, and twist down toward the floor.

Drowning

• THE TWIST — Chubby Checker's famous dance that is basically accomplished by planting your feet and twisting back and forth on the balls of them.

The Twist

• TRAVELING ARMS — This is taken from the referee's signal in a basketball game that indicates a "traveling" infraction. Great for samba, conga and even rock and roll music.

Traveling arms

• PATTY-CAKE — Like the child's game, variations of this clapping and slapping pattern can add a real spark to riser choreography. Like "giving 10" or "slipping some skin" or even a "high five" are all closely related and provide some fun ideas for staging.

Patty-cake

• WAVING — Wave your hand overhead. Slow, fast, one hand or both.

Waving

• FINGER SNAPS — There are lots of variations of finger snaps, from simply back and forth at waist level, to up and down at your sides or overhead, one hand, two hands, etc. You never have to move a foot.

Finger snaps

PRESENT ARMS — This refers to arm positions like a game show host "presenting" the prize. (See description and pictures in STEP ONE of GOTTA SING GOTTA DANCE)

1 low
2 high
3 moving low to high
4 burst
5 alternating positions
6 present "L" arms

• MANY ARMS/ONE BODY — This is a visual look that happens when two or more performers line up, one behind the other, and present their arms at different levels so that it looks like one body has many arms.

Many arms/one body

• "S" POSE — Mainly a feminine pose where the girls stand with their feet together, one knee bent in front of the other, shoulders square to the audience. This is a stance used by show girls and models because it presents a very attractive line to the body.

"S Pose"

• KNEE POPS — More masculine than an "S" pose, feet are in a wide second position. The dancer simply pops his knees forward by quickly lifting his heels off the floor. The dancers head should stay at one level through out.

Knee pops

• WALKING KNEE POPS — Feet together, the knees are bent alternately as though the dancer were walking down the street.

Walking knee pops

• COUNTRY KNEE SLAPS — Knees turned out, elbows out to the side, the dancers slap their thighs on beats two and four, or walk with fists and elbows working to the side like a bow-legged cowboy.

Country knee slaps

• BELL ARMS — This is a swinging motion of the arms like the pendulum of a bell. This can be done holding hands with a partner or in a long line of performers. A common pattern is to swing them one fourth of the way up and then back down to the sides. Then swing them halfway up and then down. Then three fourths of the way and down and eventually all the way up. It can be both a very happy move or one that suggests brotherhood and unity.

See the musical example from "It's Christmas Time" by Urselene McCamley and from the revue ALL AMERICAN arranged by Mark Brymer on the video.

• SWAYS — Swaying is not as easy as it might sound, especially for young performers. One thing that might help is to think of leading from side to side with your leading shoulder. In other words, as you sway to the left, your left shoulder is the first to get there, then the rest of the body follows. This is the same whether the performers are standing or sitting. For interest's sake, try having the cast all sway in one direction for a while, then have every other line sway the opposite direction. Try swaying with your hands behind your backs, or up in front of your shoulders with spread jazz hands.

Sways

• ROCKING HEADS — Sometimes a move as simple as tilting your head from side to side like a metronome can be just the right visual effect for a number. It need not be a big move at all to look happy or even just "simple."

See the musical example "Happy Music In The Air" by Ruth Artman on the video.

• HAND JIVE — This is another 1950s and '60s routine that consists of sixteen counts of slaps, claps and other hand movements.

1 & 2	slap thighs two times
3 & 4	clap two times
5 & 6	wipe one hand over the other two times
7 & 8	wipe other hand over the other two times
9 & 10	pound right fist on top of the other two times
11 & 12	pound left fist on top of the other two times
13 & 14	motion right thumb over right shoulder two times
15 & 16	motion left thumb over left shoulder two times.

• THE MONKEY — A dance in which the dancers move their arms up and down in alternation like a monkey climbing a tree.

The Monkey

CHOOSING THE MUSIC

Here are some very basic things to keep in mind when you are choosing the music that you want to add movement to with younger performers.

•Keep in mind how much repetition will be necessary. Will you still find the music interesting after long and repetitive rehearsals? Will the movement be as repetitive as the music? This can be O.K. and sometimes preferable, but you need to be able to find music that will hold both you and your audience's interest. If you are thinking that the choreography or staging will "save" a weak musical number, you should probably reconsider your choice. Bad music is just bad. You can't cover it up with all of the clever staging and gimmickry in the world. There's a lot of good music out there. Go ahead and be particular!

• Is there enough variety and rhythmic interest to keep the music rewarding for the long haul? You are going to have to live with this music for a long time. Make sure that you and your performers like it. There will probably be a variety of levels of difficulty as well. If everything is either too easy or too difficult the process of putting it together could turn frustrating for everyone. A mixture is probably the best way to go. You want to have a good balance of music that allows for quick success and repertoire that challenges and stretches all involved. In the end, those more challenging numbers will usually have the lasting qualities.

• Make certain that the lyrics and the message of the songs you select are suitable for your young performers. This goes for costume and staging choices as well. There is no reason to try to make Las Vegas showgirls out of your fifth grade girls choir! Let the beauty and freshness of the young shine through your repertoire and staging choices.

• Your musical and staging choices will be effected by the size of your cast as well. The good news is that it is very often easier to do choreography with a large group than a very small one. If a big group of performers does a little move it looks like a lot happened, the effect can be quite dramatic even if the move was not. A small group performing the same move will have a relatively small effect. To get the same amount of impact they may actually have to do more. This puts more pressure on each individual performer. In other words, when it comes to doing choreography, "the more performers, the merrier" is often a very accurate statement.

SIMPLE DANCE STEPS – After you have exhausted your vocabulary of dance steps that involve no feet movement you might want to move onto some very simple dance steps that are very accessible to young dancers. At this point you might want to go back to STEP 1 — GOTTA SING GOTTA DANCE and start from square one. You recall that this square is simply "walking." Then, like you would with more mature dancers, you can move on to marching, step touching, step kicking, different patterns on the floor like box steps and pivots, stylized marches and walks like "country," "swing," "funk," and all of the others.

THE PROCESS OF TEACHING STEPS — One of the most effective ways of teach dance steps to young performers is to learn the steps with their hands before they make the transfer to their feet. At a young age it is often easier to manipulate the hands as opposed to those feet that seem so far away. Get right down on the floor and try a few steps with your hands instead of your feet. Start with walking. Then go to box steps, soft shoe, step touching, Charleston, step kicking. After each step is practiced with your hands, stand and replace the hands with your feet keeping your eyes on the places where your hands were once doing the walking.

Learning the steps with the hands

See the musical example from "Happy Music In The Air" by Ruth Artman and "Bill Bailey Won't You Please Come Home" from "Dixieland Jamboree" arranged by Kirby Shaw on the video.

DECISIONS! DECISIONS!

Here are some choices and approaches to movement that are left up to the director.

• KEEP LIKE VOICE PARTS TOGETHER — This is especially true with younger performers who still feel safety in numbers. You can often teach appropriate choreography that will reflect individual voice parts especially on partner songs and beginning two and three part work.

• DEVELOP INTERESTING "TRAFFIC" PATTERNS ON STAGE — Traffic is the movement of the cast around the stage. Sometimes you can make the stage visually exciting without performing any real dance steps. Instead you can experiment with patterns of movement around the stage, for instance, lines moving in opposition, circles inside the other and moving in opposite directions, lines intersecting one another like a "meat grinder," and just simply walking from one position to another with interesting routes.

See the musical example "When The Saints Go Marching In" from "Dixieland Jamboree" arranged by Kirby Shaw.

• PEEL-OFF SEQUENCES — This means to take one move and have it performed in succession from one end of the choir to the other. Peel-offs are fun to watch and what's more, they use up a lot of counts! Try them with individuals, with voice parts, rows, or any other size groups. Four groups often work for a song based on four bar phrases, but there are many other interesting variations for peel-offs and waves.

Try a move as simple as a salute, a wave of the hand or a clap for your first experiments with peel offs. Later try moves that require several beats for each group to accomplish.

• "MIRRORING" — Young students can sometimes find mirroring by the director to be quite helpful. At the very least, the director can help get the group started in the right direction. You can also keep reassuring eye contact with them throughout their performance. Maybe you'll want to mirror only in rehearsal situations, depending really upon the experience level of your cast. Or you may want to help your gang out even in performance. You will be surprised how unobtrusive you really are, even if you feel huge dancing in front of your group with your back to the audience. Parents and other relatives have a great ability to see right through you and spy their little star in the third row! For older performers, "mirroring" can sometimes be too confusing to be worth your effort. There will be some who are trying to second guess you. This could lead to unneeded frustration. For these older performers you may want to just teach the number facing the same direction they are facing. Later, when you want to watch their progress, you can turn around and do so after they have had some time for the routines to sink in. Again, much of this will depend on your own teaching style and the experience level of your cast.

• DEMONSTRATE WITH FULL ENERGY — It is important that the choreographer always demonstrate a move with full energy and intensity. You can never tell when any of your individual cast members is going to "get it" this time. You want to make sure they see what you want and do not have to interpret your intentions. Every time you demonstrate a move another cast member might be more or less tuned in to you than the last time. You need to give it your all so that they will too.

SPECIAL DETAILS

Everybody loves to go to Disneyland! It is the creme de la creme of theme parks and entertainment venues of all kinds. The reason for this is because the producers of the Disney Magic pay excruciating attention to details. The stanchions at the haunted mansion have gargoyles on their tops. The trash cans in Frontierland are shaped and painted like logs in a forest and the butter patties in the Main Street Cafeteria have Mickey Mouse ears embossed in them. When guests go home from Disneyland it is true that they remember the thrill of Space Mountain and the wonder of It's A Small World." But, what really impresses them the most is that someone cared enough about their patronage to put Mickey Mouse Ears in the butter patties!

Your performances, no matter how modest, will be greatly enhanced by the amount of time you spend on the intricate details that make your show special. This is such an important part of your efforts.

• TRANSITIONS — This is an area that will show your attention to detail. It is also the area where you will show off your rough edges if you do not spend the time and energy on them. You should time your transitions to make them efficient. You should rework them to make them entertaining and musical in their own right. Can you use a reprise of the previous song to make the transition? Can you use the introduction of the next selection to make your transition? Can you come up with a musical motif that can recur throughout the performance? Is there a related piece of music that will help set up the next number? Should there be dialogue between numbers? A skit? A poem?

• BOWS — Bows are another area of detail that must be addressed and rehearsed. Here are a few rules to consider:

Most bows should be executed with your feet absolutely together. Not even one inch apart. There are several kinds and tempos of bows that will send a different kind of "thank you" to your audience.

(1) A very youthful and energetic bow includes rising up on your toes on beat four, bowing low and letting your hands drop toward the floor for beats 5 & 6. On 7, you stand again and raise up onto your toes. Then on beat 8 you lower yourself back to the floor, stand still and smile. This bow can be accomplished at almost any tempo, usually relative to the number that you have just finished.

(2) A more formal bow would have the performers lift their chins slightly just before they bow and keep their face toward the audience until they are about half way down to their full bow.

(3) It is generally agreed that the deeper the bow the more formal, however, sometimes just a simple nod of the head will seem appropriate.

(4) Audience applause should almost always be acknowledged by the performers.

(5) A disciplined cast can often be led through bows by the director or a lead dancer on stage. This will leave you the flexibility to bow more and differently in response to different kinds of audience response. Usually the simple flip of the directors hand is enough of a signal to alert a well rehearsed ensemble. The director can flip their hand at the tempo they feel the bow should be executed.

(6) A fun bow that appears more choreographed is the "peel off" or "ripple" bow where the performers go down and up like dominoes.

For a musical example see the revue ALL-AMERICAN arranged by Mark Brymer on the video.

DISCIPLINE

Discipline is always very impressive and should also be rehearsed. With young performers, it is often a good idea to set a "stand-by" or "attention" position that signals that the cast is ready to concentrate either for the upcoming rehearsal or performance. One possibility is to have all of the performers stand with their feet together and hands held in the small of their backs. Notice how there is space at the rib cage level. This is a very clean and disciplined line from whence to begin. It can, however, cause some tension across the rib cage and shoulders which is not good for singing. However, as a starting position it works very well.

Stand-by -1

Zero position

Stand-by - 2

ZERO POSITION — This is the stance most comfortable to most. Feet slightly apart, arms dangling at your sides, shoulders low and relaxed. From here choreography begins.

FIDGETING HANDS — The first place that discipline tends to fall apart with young performers is with their hands. It is hard to know what to do with them especially in front of a crowd. Even adults commonly have this problem. The key is to give them definite assignments. Held at your sides, in the small of your back, clasped in front of your waist, on your hips or even grabbing the seam of your pants are all valid possibilities. Just give them a specific assignment so that there is no temptation to wander!

HARNESS THAT ENERGY! — The great thing about working with young performers is their limitless energy. Dance is a way of putting that energy to positive use. It is not a replacement for good singing! It's simply a way of making a good performance newly effective and in a different way! You need not be intimidated. You merely need to start simply and grow, the same way you did when you started to develop your musical skills.

CONCLUSION

Most people who will be reading this book will probably be using music and dance in circles of education and amateur artistic endeavors. That is where much of the dynamic growth in song, dance and entertainment is taking place. It would be easy to pontificate about the many benefits that including singing and dancing in our educational settings present. They are broad and legitimate. Most of the performers involved in these endeavors will not go on to make singing and dancing a lifetime career even though some most definitely will. But every one of the people that are involved in these kinds of projects will come away with at least a few valuable tools and lessons.

They will have better posture.

They will be able to present themselves with a greater air of confidence.

They will experience the basic emotions and passions musicality affords them.

They will discover ways to express themselves more creatively and effectively.

They will present themselves to the rest of the world in a positive frame of reference.

They will hone priceless motor skills that will stay with them for their entire life.

They will experience and learn team work, responsibility, stamina, enthusiasm, tenderness, passion, problem- and crisis-solving and a more sensitive awareness of the world around them.

These skills, taught early will stay with an individual for a very long time and truly will make them better musicians, at least, and better human beings at best! Besides that... it's fun!

A special note of thanks to a fine director and music educator Debbie Moyers and to her students from Garfield High School in Virginia for serving as models for this book.

Cover photo: New London, Wisconsin, Jr./Sr. High music students, LuAnn Rupnow and Lori Flury, directors.

Ed Goewey, Jennifer Griffin, Jessica Jackson, Emily Suzanne Jolly,
Brad MacMullen, Delante McCreary, Latrina Miller, Marcellus F. Stuck III,
Christine Marie West, Jonathan Dominick West, Melissa K. Wilhoit

Chris Ahr, Jessie Raskin, Francesca Watson, Dericka Scott, Taishia Gardner

TO BE A TEACHER - JOHN JACOBSON
Motivational Cassette Series for Music Teachers

Beyond his gifts as an educator and choreographer, John Jacobson has the gift of motivation, not only for students, but for their teachers as well! Now you can enjoy John's inspiring message in the car, before, after, or during school, or anytime you need a lift!

Each of the four (all new) 30-minute topics explores an area of interest to music teachers, giving encouragement and practical tips to help you achieve your musical and professional goals. Topics include:

1. If It Ain't Got Heart, It Ain't Art
2. Music Makes The Difference - Justifying Your Program
3. Climb Every Mountain
4. To Be A Teacher

08602156 Cassette Pak (2) $14.95

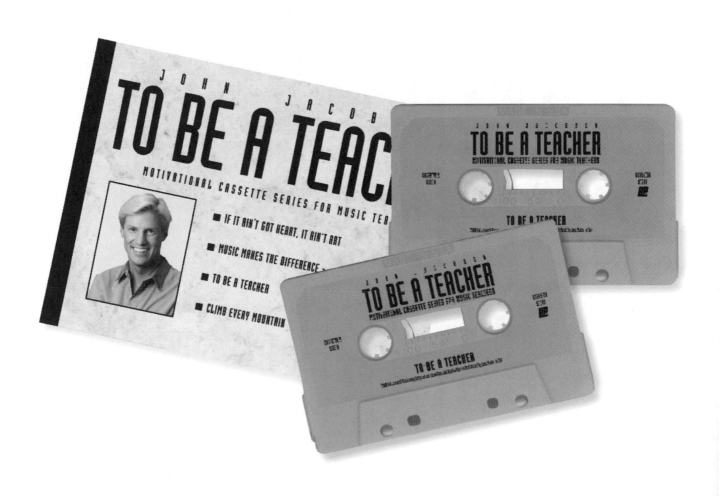

EXCERPTS FROM

JOHN JACOBSON'S RISER CHOREOGRAPHY
A Director's Guide For Enhancing Choral Performances

Movement enhances even the simplest of musical settings. It can bring energy to a dynamic show choir number or simple elegance to a beautiful concert piece without your choir ever leaving the risers! John Jacobson's ideas for staging and choreography on choral risers have been compiled in this easy-to-use resource for the beginning or veteran choral director. Covering basic formations, visual effect, and simple gestures that enhance the lyrics, this practical guide will help you incorporate all kinds of staging into your performance.

08745827 Book $12.95
08745828 Video.....................................$29.95
08745829 Book/Video Pak $34.95

QUESTION #1:

Where Do I Begin?

Let's take it from where we're "AT."

FILING ON

Notice how much nicer it appears to the audience if, when your choir is walking on, you send the front row first as opposed to the back row. In this way, the natural adjusting and shuffling that needs to happen is somewhat camouflaged by an already-in-place front row.

Front row stationary while back rows file on

It is sometimes a safe idea to have the top row walk first to the next-to-the-top level and then step up all at once.

Top row walks to second step, then all step up to third step

If you have the luxury of being able to enter from both sides of the stage you can obviously get your choir in place twice as fast by sending one row from each side. Try sending rows one and three from one side and two and four from the other.

First and third rows enter from right, second and fourth rows enter from left

Try having two rows enter from each side at the same time to cut down your entrance time by a huge amount.

If you have the luxury of having extra choral risers try setting them up as steps going off the back of the top riser. See how dramatic an entrance can be made by having all or some of your choir enter en masse up and over from behind.

Entering from behind the risers

With this same arrangement you could enter a row or two from each side, plus one or two up and over the back for a rapid and dramatic entrance.

Front two rows entering from sides, back two rows enter from behind

---

If you have the facility, try having your rows enter from all over the auditorium at once. Through the audience, from the wings, up and over the back of the risers are all effective entrances.

Entering from all over the auditorium

THE SCRAMBLE

This is a way of mounting the risers that says to your choir, "You've got this much time to get there, now get there." This should be used for a very quick entrance that will surprise your audience and let them know that they are in for something different and unpredictable. The choir members could come from anywhere in the auditorium, or from off stage, including perhaps even from audience chairs.

The scramble

You may even try the SCRAMBLE type entrance using music from the first song of your performance. This would work for a slow song that needs to build or the introduction or first verse of an up-tempo song. It would even be effective to enter from all over the place singing a traditional madrigal processional selection.

QUESTION #2:

O.K. You're There, Now What?

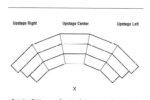

Upstage Right   Upstage Center   Upstage Left

X

Downstage Right   Downstage Center   Downstage Left

Stage areas

BLOCK FORMATION

The most traditional choice is to have the entire block choir focus their eyes on the director so that he/she can truly lead them through the musical selection. The cleanest way to have your choir stand is with their outside foot slightly forward and pointing at the director. Those on stage right will have their right foot forward. Those on stage left will have their left foot forward. This gives a very unifying "line" to each individual's body and to the group as a whole. This is called a "closed" position.

Choir in closed position